BASE NOTES

Adelle Stripe is an author, poet and journalist based in Calderdale, West Yorkshire. Her books include the *Sunday Times* bestseller *Ten Thousand Apologies*, and *Black Teeth and a Brilliant Smile*, a fictionalised biography inspired by the playwright Andrea Dunbar. She was shortlisted for the Gordon Burn Prize, Portico Prize for Literature and Penderyn Music Book Prize. As a journalist, she has contributed to *The Quietus*, *New Statesman*, *Record Collector* and *Yorkshire Post*. She is a recipient of Manchester University's Anthony Burgess Fellowship.

BASE NOTES
THE SCENTS OF A LIFE

◇─────────◇

Adelle Stripe

WHITE RABBIT

First published in Great Britain in 2025 by White Rabbit
an imprint of The Orion Publishing Group Ltd
Carmelite House, 50 Victoria Embankment
London EC4Y 0DZ

An Hachette UK Company

The authorised representative in the EEA is Hachette Ireland,
8 Castlecourt Centre, Castleknock Road, Dublin 15, D15 XTP3,
Republic of Ireland (email: info@hbgi.ie)

1 3 5 7 9 10 8 6 4 2

Copyright © Adelle Stripe 2025

The moral right of Adelle Stripe to be identified as
the author of this work has been asserted in accordance
with the Copyright, Designs and Patents Act of 1988.

All rights reserved. No part of this publication may be
reproduced, stored in a retrieval system, or transmitted
in any form or by any means, electronic, mechanical,
photocopying, recording, or otherwise, without the
prior permission of both the copyright owner and the
above publisher of this book.

A CIP catalogue record for this book is
available from the British Library.

ISBN Hardback 9781399608602
ISBN eBook 9781399608633
ISBN Audio 9781399608640

Typeset by Input Data Services Ltd, Bridgwater, Somerset

Printed in Great Britain by Clays Ltd, Elcograf, S.p,A.

www.whitcrabbitbooks.co.uk
www.orionbooks.co.uk

For Katy

Contents

Rive Gauche	1
4711	9
Giorgio Beverly Hills	33
Dewberry	53
Trésor	65
CK One	77
Le Male	93
Angel	107
Earthworm	123
Brut	147
L'Eau D'Issey	163
Happy	179
Hugo	193
Dune	209
Original Musk	221
Old Spice	231
Red Door	243
Lune Rose	257
Acknowledgements	275

RIVE GAUCHE

Yves Saint Laurent

On her slender wrist, a solid gold bracelet. IKB silk. Shoulder pads high. Vermilion lips. Water wave clips. She is holding a pen, making big decisions. On the table, a glass of Beaujolais Nouveau. Men whisper to her in this Left Bank café. Smoking a chain of sleek cigarettes. Leather gloves draped over a book. Garter stockings. Legs ajar. Knotted sling-ons shine in the light…

As the car crawls towards the city centre, you stare up at looming chimneys, textile mills and minarets silhouetted on the horizon. The sky bleeds orange in Bradford. This is not like the place where you live, a town many miles away with flat fields, breweries and thick clouds of malt hanging over the rooftops. Your mother has driven you here after watching the Winter Olympics. It is the only ice rink in West Yorkshire, and already you are excited. After badgering her all week, she has agreed to teach you how to skate.

There is a queue outside the concrete building when you arrive, so before parking up, she drives up the hill and stops outside a supermarket, with rows of fruit and vegetables, the likes of which you have never seen before. Reading the signs for red peppers and jackfruit, you wonder what they taste like. Your mother says it's the only place she can buy lychees, unless she orders them from the Chinese takeaway as a pudding with condensed milk, so she buys a small wooden box from a woman in a yellow sari and brings them back into the car. Together, you crack open the honeycomb shells as their sweet smell fills the air. She pulls a funny face and tells you it's like eating an eyeball, albeit a tasty one. Juice dribbles down your chin; she leans over to wipe it with a stiff pocket tissue. Then you clean your hands as she starts up the engine. This is her latest fast car, a red Ford Granada Mark II. She thinks it's her passport to freedom.

After parking up behind the sign for Silver Blades, you walk up the stairwell with names carved into the banister by compass and penknife, then buy tickets from the kiosk. The man behind the

BASE NOTES

glass with a drooping cigarette in his mouth says the venue has never been as busy, not since Torvill & Dean danced in Sarajevo. Your mother replies to him saying that's why she's come. A new career beckons for her. He starts to smile as she talks to him. 'I'm not joking either! There's a leopard print leotard in this bag. Is there much call for overweight women on ice?'

Your mother has a way of making everyone laugh, especially men. It is one of her special skills. Together you laugh a lot. Sometimes she pulls a Cissie & Ada face if you are being too serious. Sometimes you laugh at things that are awful. Sometimes until your belly hurts. Both of you adore slapstick. Especially when it happens in real life, laughing at the physical misfortune of others. Everyone in your family is the same. Your sense of humour often gets you into trouble.

From behind the barrier, you hear the city's kids skate quickly around the rink. It is a struggle to tie up your boots. Your mother leans over to double knot the laces, pulls on your gloves and tells you to go slow. She is wearing an emerald dress with puffed sleeves and matching eyeshadow to bring out the colour in her eyes. They are pale green with tiny brown freckles, yours are a dull shade of brown that turn Lucozade orange in the right kind of light.

Before leaving the house, your mother painted her nails and blow-dried her hair, which is three tints of red – maroon, mahogany and copper – with a butterscotch flash in the fringe. Her hair is sprayed with multiple coats of Elnett Strong Hold to fix it in place. She wants to look glamorous on ice.

Swaying through the gate, her perfume fills the air; it is the familiar scent of Rive Gauche. Iris, peach and honeysuckle . . . bergamot, ylang-ylang . . . jasmine . . . gardenia . . . oakmoss . . . vetiver . . . sandalwood . . . musk . . . She keeps the black and blue bottle on her bedside table that is always coated in talcum powder dust.

Her perfumes are mysterious concoctions, and when she isn't looking, sometimes you make your own cocktail from squirting the liquids together in the palm of your hand, then splash the homemade scent onto your neck. Entering her bedroom without asking is against the rules, but rooting around in there when she's busy cutting hair in the kitchen is the only way to find clues about how to be a woman. Already you are anxious about the puzzling objects concealed in her drawers, the white cotton tubes, lacy knickers with elastic bits, or the book beneath her bed with fishnet stockings on the front. You already know that in a few years' time your body will change, then you will be forced to become a teenage girl. After that, a wife, then a mother. Already your future has been planned out. There is not much choice about what to become in the small town where you live.

Stepping onto the ice, the little skaters bounce up and down as music booms from speaker cabinets. You are excited or scared and can't decide which this feeling is. There is nowhere like this at home. Bradford's children can dance and move in a way that you've never seen before. Some speak in languages that are unfamiliar. At your school, everyone has white skin, and all the children talk the same, in a strange, meandering accent with elongated vowels stretching out into the barley fields.

Your mother takes hold of your hand and coaxes you away from the barrier, her breath leaves a trail of frozen words behind her as she pushes her legs in motion.

'Let go and move!' she says. 'Relax into it, like this . . .'

Nothing seems to frighten her. And even though she is clumsy like you, on the ice she seems to be graceful, as if she is floating, weightless, almost flying. She has not looked this carefree in a long time.

You hear her say, 'I've forgotten all my troubles already . . .'

Back home, your mother cries a lot, about her body, her dead brother, mean customers at work, your father's obsession with his cows and often about you. Her firstborn is not turning out quite like she expected. Already you are *too much of a deep thinker*. All she ever wanted was a normal daughter, one like the other girls in town, but instead she has ended up with you, a child who was suspended from school for biting another girl's face, a child who cannot comprehend numbers, a child who believes she can levitate and see ghosts and predict the future. A child who is not quite right.

Clinging to her hand and stepping reluctantly onto the ice, you hope this time you won't slip and end up with sliced fingers like Struwwelpeter. Onstage, a DJ wearing aviator sunglasses plays records with mobile disco lights in red and blue with flashing strobes. He has a smoke machine behind him belching out a puff of dry ice onto the real ice with each new record he selects. By now, you are learning to balance and have started to pick up speed as he plays 'Agadoo' at full blast. Rocking your body from side to side, you sway into the knees, just like your mother tells you to do.

Then there is a crackle from the speakers, and the skaters turn silent. The DJ announces the next record on the microphone, dedicating the song to 'all you Torvill & Dean fans out there'. Your mother lets out a very loud 'woo-hoo!' which echoes up to the ceiling. You have only just started noticing how embarrassing she is compared to all the other mums. As your cheeks turn red, she starts skating in circles under the spotlight in her long, ruffled dress. You shrink back, pretending she's a stranger, even when she waves.

RIVE GAUCHE

As the drums on Ravel's *Boléro* pick up speed, she accelerates in loops around the rink. You watch her try to move like a competition skater, spinning and wobbling in time to the music. The skaters on the rink are laughing at her now because she is loud, because of her clothes, because she is heavy. They start to link arms, all of them moving quickly, faster, flashing past you in a blur. For a moment you are lost, unable to see her; a haze of CO_2 and Impulse body mist fills the refrigerated air as girls with home perms and pink pearl lipstick start spinning to the crescendo.

And then the music stops. The needle scratches to an empty hum. And you are overwhelmed by people rushing towards the sound of screaming. It is a sound you recognise. It is the sound of your mother. You cannot reach her for the adults but can hear her pleading for help.

Peering through the adults' legs, you push towards her on the ice. Her dress has turned upside down like a broken umbrella in a storm and you can see her big bum, torn tights and knickers. You don't know what to do. You think she is joking. Just like the people on TV. Then you start to laugh, thinking it's one of her practical jokes. But the laughing soon stops as everyone stares and you see her hyperventilating on the glaze. Her leg swells up to twice the size. It takes three ambulance men to roll her onto a stretcher and wheels when they arrive.

After the hall has emptied of people, it's just you alone on the ice. It is almost dark outside; the lights are still flashing to a silent disco. Gulping a mouthful of worry, you overhear the paramedics telling her not to panic, that the pain will be over soon as they fix a brace onto her expanding calf before moving her. The old man from the kiosk unlaces the skating boots from her feet, reaching his hand towards hers in the chaos.

BASE NOTES

Leaning over the barrier, you hear them say she has smashed her leg in two places as she pleads with them to make the swelling stop. 'Not long now,' they say. 'We're taking you straight to Smith Lane.' As you skate out alone beneath the spotlights, you realise you are finally able to move on your own. Her wailing echoes behind you.

With your hands covering your ears, you start singing to yourself, moving gracefully at last towards the centre of the ice. Staring down at your boots, you wonder if their blades will catch on a crack, but it is smooth underfoot, almost like glass.

4711

Mäurer & Wirtz

Domestic perfection, a gleaming nest. Adoring children with Aryan hair. A waist small enough for her husband's grasp. He arrives home at dusk. Dinner on the table. Cobalt eyes. Peep-toe courts. Easy listening drifts through the air. Her make-up applied twice already today. He speaks of the office, the money he'll make. White dress gloves, a twinset and pearls. At night, they sleep in separate beds…

After two hours of sitting in the back seat with air conditioning blasting towards your face, you are still feeling nauseous. The snaking roads make your stomach jump, and already you can taste the salty coastal breeze, although even with the windows down this isn't enough to stop the retching. It will not be long before you reach the town where your grandparents live. Outside, ditches and windmills flash past the car, as your mother sings the road sign to 'Thorngumbald' as 'Thorngingumbald!' in a silly, goonish tone, one that she hopes will make you feel excited about the oncoming summer holiday, a holiday which you always dread.

'Muuuum,' you ask, with a sorrowful, annoying whimper. 'Are you going to stay with me? You haven't got a suitcase, but I have.'

'I've work to do, so you'll stay with your grandma for a few weeks, then I'll come back and get you.'

'But I don't wanna go. It's 'orrible there. Can't I stay on my own instead?'

Letting out an exasperated sigh, your mother rolls her eyes and glares at you through the rear-view mirror.

'It's *want* to. Not *wanna*. And *horrible*, not *'orrible*. Stop dropping your aitches. It makes you sound common, like all the rest. Look, you know it's school holidays. I'm busy in the salon. Your father's milking on the farm so you must stay with Grandma. I've already to pay for your sister to be looked after because she's a baby. We can't afford another sitter.'

A warm rush of tears fills your eyes as you try to hold them back, swallowing the upset down the back of your throat.

BASE NOTES

With a sympathetic timbre, she says, 'Why don't you write a postcard . . . and tell me just how you're getting along? Send it from the promenade letterbox. I'll call every night to see how you are.'

For a few minutes you fall silent as she rummages in the car door for a cassette, then pushes Heaven 17 into the radio's mouth, turning up the volume to drown out your complaining. Above the windscreen mirror, a Little Tree oscillates, its pine fragrance almost masking the rising stench of last week's vomit that is still soaked into the seat. No matter how hard your mother has tried to scrub it out, the acidic stink from deep inside your gut is impossible to remove.

As the blaring speakers play the tape at a volume so loud it makes your ears crackle, she starts to sing along then shouts over her shoulder, 'Can you see the lighthouse yet?'

Sea fret rolls across the fields ahead, as if the whole town is burning and smoke is filling the air. Peering out from behind the car seat, you stare towards the town, and there it is, standing tall, the only high building after Hull, and one cleaned by your grandmother, who polishes the lamp each week, a lamp that hasn't worked for years, as if her sweating tears to make it sparkle will finally capture God's attention.

When the car pulls into your grandmother's drive, you can feel your pulse pumping hard as a sense of foreboding runs through your body and pools in the footwell below. It is almost as if your Jelly Bean sandals are glued to the vehicle. Your mother turns the engine off as the garden gate clanks open. Then the latch rattles, and your grandmother's face appears at the car window.

'No need to look so sulky, miss!' she laughs, with her fingers tapping against the glass, her words holding an element of

4711

wickedness that always make you wonder if she is telling the truth, trying to joke, or hiding something sinister behind her words.

You unfasten the seat belt, as she pulls you from the car, wraps her arms around you and squeezes until you can hardly breathe. Today, she is wearing a patterned nylon dress with a pussy bow collar, a kitchen apron, a heavily tinted and neatly back-combed shampoo and set, and a liberal dousing of 4711. Basil and bergamot . . . lemon . . . peach . . . oakmoss . . . cyclamen . . . vetiver . . . rose . . . patchouli and musk . . . cedar . . . oranges . . . The fragrance reminds you of mosquito candles in Spain, the place where you wish you were right now, instead of being here.

Although you have no choice about where to go on holiday, rather than facing abandonment at your grandmother's house, you imagine being transported back to the Hotel Cervantes where you swam in a pool on the rooftop last summer, ate paprika crisps and drank fizzy pop all day long in the Spanish sunshine. Although your mother left you alone in the room at night, and waited for you to fall asleep, before creeping out wearing high heels and shoulderless outfits for the nightclubs and cocktail bars, to begin with you didn't mind the solitude so much. Later, when you started to cry in the middle of the night because she hadn't returned, a maid would always try to comfort you in a language you did not understand.

Back then, it was just you and her. Before your sister was born, you often went on adventures together, never telling your father where you had been. Her leaving you alone on holiday was one of many shrouded moments. In return for your silence, she rewarded you with new clothes, trips to the Flying Pizza, and sometimes a ride on the fastest train in Britain, an InterCity 125.

BASE NOTES

Although you are only eight, you have already learnt that keeping your mouth shut and not asking questions is a way of having a better life.

Since your sister arrived, the baby has screamed all night, most nights, and even on school nights. You are no longer the centre of the universe, and no longer the cute one. Everybody is interested in the baby and not in you. For a while, you started to sulk, but at least your parents let you name her. It was agreed that if it was a boy, he'd be called Joseph, after your father's uncle who was decapitated at Rotherham Steel Works. But if a girl appeared, it would be your choice, so after coming up with a list of all the horrible names you could think of – Griselda, Ethel, Joyce or Bertha – you decided to name her after the bitter invalid in your favourite book, *What Katy Did*. Seeing as your mother hadn't read the book, or hardly any book for that matter, she had no idea about the mean trick you had just pulled. It felt like a small victory.

Running into the backyard, you immediately head towards the shed, where you know your grandfather will be hiding. He locks himself inside for a few hours every day. It is the only room in the house he has the sole key for. Inside the shed are handmade wooden boxes and drawers, with nails and drill parts, cloths and varnishes, tools and paint pots stacked on the shelves. There is a high seat from a factory workshop, and a box where he hides his lighter. By the window are three large jugs with stoppers, containing his latest effort to brew beer.

You knock on the door once, twice, three times, until he jumps out behind you from the greenhouse, shouting 'hello flower!' and you start screaming as he attempts to cause you death by a thousand nips. His hands smell of tomato leaves, his hair of old Brylcreem, his breath of bitter, his skin of wax and nicotine. And

4711

you wriggle out from his chunky bricklayer's arms, as he chases you into the house. He is all dressed up for your visit, wearing a pressed shirt and tie, cufflinks, sovereign rings and a sapphire tie-pin, with his hair greased back in a ducktail.

Inside the house, there is a new addition to his hobby collection which he is keen to show you: a Yamaha E45 organ in mahogany.

'What is that?' you ask. 'Can I have a go?'

Your grandfather picks you up onto the stool, switches on the great machine, and you stare up at the rows of keys with levers, with buttons and dials above them.

'I feel like I'm on *Top of the Pops*,' you say, before randomly hitting each bum note for too long, making a noise so dreadful that a pair of cushioned Pioneers is clamped over your ears and plugged into the jack to stop the din.

For a few minutes you pull every lever, before pausing. Through muffled headphones, you can hear your grandmother arguing with your mother in the front room. They have closed the door, but even with pots boiling on the stove, and your grandfather's whistling, you can feel something isn't right in the house. Every time your mother sees her, they end up having words. Words that often escalate into horrendous arguments that make your mother cry. It has always been like this. You pretend you are listening to your grandfather who is asking about school and your friends, but you can also tune in and hear what your grandmother is saying in the other room at the same time, words like 'you don't deserve forgiveness', 'no daughter of mine' and 'that dress is looking tight'. The familiar sound of your mother's sobbing fills the air, until the door opens, and your grandmother races through into the kitchen, her chin held high from the latest victory she has delivered over her errant firstborn daughter, the one who never lived up to her expectations.

BASE NOTES

On the kitchen table, each placemat is set with a folded napkin, and you sit in your usual spot, looking out onto the street beyond the lace net curtains. The walls are decorated with spongy Anaglypta, which you like to pick at when nobody is watching. There are pictures made from embroidery hung above the doorway, scenes of tropical beaches, snow-capped mountains and smouldering sunsets. And framed postcards of every holiday destination your grandparents have been to: Skegness, Blackpool, Scarborough, Morecambe and Rhyl. A large teak cabinet contains your grandmother's library, with books mostly from the Watch Tower. According to her, the only book anyone needs to read in its entirety is the Bible. Every morning, she flicks through passages and makes notes, then compares them to articles in the magazine which she tries to push into people's hands on doorsteps around town.

When she's out preaching, your grandfather quietly sits on his comfy chair, surrounded by balls of silk, crochet hooks and patterns ordered through the post. Since having a stroke and losing all feeling on one side, crochet has helped bring back movement in his body. He has made over ten giant tablecloths with patterns of roses, peacock feathers and paisley. Creating delicate, beautiful things is not what people expected from a strapping builder like him. They are dipped in sugar water to preserve the shape.

As your grandmother rattles a baking tray from the oven, you ask, 'When are we having lunch?'

'You're always hungry, aren't you?' she replies. 'Eyes bigger than your belly.'

Hanging your head, you stare down at the patterned carpet, kicking your feet against the chair legs.

'Don't kick the chair!'

'I'm not.'

4711

'If you're telling lies, then Jehovah will know. He sees everything.'

Together, you all sit around the table and say grace. Everyone else's heads are lowered as they mumble a prayer. Instead of saying the words, you remain quiet and stare at the pile of watery cabbage, carrot mash, boiled potatoes and dry roast chicken, slices of bread and marge, the jug of instant gravy and pot of tea in front of you. When your mother serves the food, she gives herself a smaller portion than yours. On her neck are red splodges from the upset.

Gravy is poured on every plate except your grandfather's. Instead of gravy, he prefers to use his own recipe, which is a pot of mashed black tea. You watch in bemusement as he pours the Ringtons loose leaf through a strainer and all over his food.

'Why are you doing that?' you ask him.

'Because out in Burma, we didn't have gravy, just tea. And since then, I've only had tea on my tea!'

'That's disgusting,' you say, as he chews the chicken with his mouth wide open. All the food is rolling between his teeth like a washing machine.

On the kitchen wall, there is a photo of him taken on shore leave in Singapore, looking handsome like a star of the big screen in wide legged trousers and a khaki slouch hat. He doesn't talk about the War very often; he says he'd rather forget about what happened in Rangoon. Especially being taken prisoner by Japanese soldiers, who only fed him rice for a month, until he escaped from the camp by swimming up the Irrawaddy, a river full of crocodiles. He has forgotten most of the Hindi he spoke with the Chindits out there. But the thing he wants to forget most is his best friend who lost his mind in the jungle, the one who his squad had to fire bullets at together to stop his strange shouting, so the Japanese hiding in the branches above wouldn't hear him and shoot all the soldiers dead. Forty years on, the memory keeps him awake at night. It is a story he cannot forget.

After lunch, you head outside into the garden and play beneath the cherry tree, a tree with sharp branches that your grandmother used to beat your mother with when she misbehaved as a teenage girl. The last time you stayed here, she told you the Bible teaches that children must be disciplined; if you strike them with a rod, they will not die, and their souls will be saved from Sheol.

Attempting to make a cartwheel beneath the tree, you collapse in a heap on the lawn, staring up at the contrails and scudding clouds that are racing across the bright blue sky. The sound of a car engine starts up as your mother's Granada vanishes down the drive, then speeds off into the distance.

Walking out from the back door, your grandfather asks, 'Why are you sad?'

'Mum didn't say goodbye.'

'That's because she didn't want to upset you. So she left by the front door instead.'

'Well, I am a bit upset.'

'Here,' he says, holding you close against him. 'I'll tell you what, tomorrow we'll have a day out and I'll take you to Muggies to play bingo.'

A smile breaks out across your face as he clasps his arms around your body.

'But one thing, flower, you know the rules . . .'

'No telling Grandma.'

'That's right,' he replies. 'She doesn't approve of gambling, or Muggies, even when it's for fun. We'll have to keep it just between ourselves.'

*

4711

The following morning you wake to the sound of a microwave humming downstairs. There is excitement in your belly at the thought of a trip to Muggies Amusement Arcade. Sitting up in bed, you pull the sheets to one side, and notice the books that were beside your bed last night are missing. You were reading *George's Marvellous Medicine* and a Marmalade Atkins annual before you fell asleep; now both have been removed and replaced with *My Book of Bible Stories*, which is bound in a yellow leather cushion cover, with red foil lettering on the front.

You open the curtains, wondering why your own books have been taken away, then start flicking through the pages of what your grandmother would rather you read instead. Inside there are coloured illustrations of Jezebel being thrown out of a window before being eaten by dogs; Jesus crucified on a stake; Stephen being stoned; King Solomon cutting a baby in two; Israelites smiling as they watch chariots drowning in the Red Sea; Cain murdering Abel; Jael lying dead in a pool of blood with a tent peg bludgeoned through his ear canal; Lot's wife being turned to salt; and Babylon the Great, sitting astride a seven-headed lion, wearing a purple Turkish belly dancer's outfit and an ankle chain. Babylon is the picture that interests you the most. All the bad women in *My Book of Bible Stories* wear slinky outfits at the temple, gold jewellery, make-up and have long, luxurious, back-combed hair. You hope one day you will look like them. Especially Delilah. If that's what hell is supposed to be, you wonder if it's the kind of place you are heading.

'Morning lazybones,' your grandmother says as you walk into the kitchen downstairs, wearing tiger feet slippers and a big fluffy dressing gown. 'Would you like some breakfast?'

'Yes please. Can I have some porridge?'

'If I make you it, you must eat it. Because you shan't be getting fed until lunch.'

BASE NOTES

'OK.'

You watch as she pours a packet of Ready Brek into a square Tupperware bowl, then empties a cup of water on top, with a shake of salt from the orange Hornsea Pottery set on the table and switches the microwave on for five minutes.

'Please can I have it with butter and milk and sugar, on a plate?'

Slamming the bowl in front of you, she says, 'You'll get what you're given.'

For a moment you stare at the hard grey mass, stirring the mixture around, sniffing at it, before attempting to swallow a spoon of the salty sludge, which has the consistency of stiff wallpaper paste.

Although your belly is rumbling, you cannot eat what has been made for you, and each time her back is turned, you spoon lumps of it into a tissue in your dressing gown pocket.

'Not hungry?'

'Sorry,' you reply, staring at the sludge. 'It doesn't taste very nice.'

Whisking the bowl away from beneath your nose, she tuts. Then, with a harshness, she mutters, 'As I said before you asked for it, there's no more food until you finish. There are children starving in Ethiopia, you know. What they'd give for that breakfast. Now hurry up and get yourself ready, I've a study class to be at this morning.'

Shovelling a scoop of sour grapefruit into her mouth from a Pyrex bowl, she rushes to the sink, then gathers her Bible notes together. After scrubbing the kitchen side with Jif, she slams the back door behind her and vanishes in a puff of smoke. You are relieved she has gone, as if the windows are finally open with fresh air flowing in.

4711

After he finishes drying the pots, your grandfather asks, 'Are you dressed, flower?'

'My belly's rumbling.'

'Tell you what, we'll stop off at the bakery and we can eat hot buttered cakes straight from the oven, on the prom. How does that sound?'

You smile at him, as he zips up your jacket.

'Pass me the stick,' he says. And you lean into the understairs cupboard, pulling out an ivory walking cane that he uses on special occasions. Your grandmother is resolute in her opinion that he doesn't require any assistance, that he's putting on his limp for sympathy, which is something he doesn't get from her, and that his stick is just attention-seeking, like the bravery medals he sometimes pins on his jacket.

Brushing down his camel coat, he straightens his tie in the mirror, and pulls on a pair of leather gloves to complete the outfit.

'Will I do?' he asks, waving his cane in the air, before locking the door, taking you by the hand, and walking you down towards the sea.

'That one looks good, Grampsy. It matches your jacket.'

Your grandfather replies with a song to his words, delivered in a cabaret style, 'I'm the best-dressed chicken in town.'

After eating a bag of steaming breadcakes you both walk along the promenade, staring out at the churning sea and the rowdy seagulls fighting over abandoned cold chips in scrunched-up newspaper balls.

'Let's go see Uncle Bert,' he says. 'He'll be over the moon to see you.'

When he answers the door, Uncle Bert's hair is longer than you remember. It has grown past his shoulders, and his skin has deepened to a dark muddy shade, from all the hours he spends on the beach sunbathing.

'Hello, young lassie,' Bert replies, as he beckons you both inside the house, a building that resembles the front of a boat peering out into the North Sea. He lives here with his brother, who has lost his memory, and has been dating your great-grandmother for fifteen years. Each night, they drink sherry in the front room, then walk for miles along the seafront. They are glad to have found each other.

Bert's living room is not like any house you have been in. It has stripped wooden floors, large kentia palms and a record player, where he listens to classical music by Mahler and Holst at full volume on Wharfedale speakers. He creates chalk drawings of naked bodies on black paper and pins them on his wall, alongside shelves stacked with books about art and poetry. At the age of eighty-two, he insists on swimming in the cold waves every day, whatever the weather.

For a reason you do not fully understand yet, he dislikes your grandmother and always says she is 'gone in the head' for believing in such mad ideas. Since last Christmas, he has refused to step foot in her house, so now you must visit him here instead. You have never met anyone quite like Bert. He is the most interesting person you know.

After finishing a glass of cream soda, which he always keeps in a bottle in the fridge, he hugs you, then pushes three pounds into your hand. Then you run along the pavement to Muggies to play on the slot machines and one-arm bandits. Taking turns on the pinball, you and your grandfather play together as the sound of Penny Falls cascade on the balcony above, a hypnotic cloud of burnt candyfloss floating in the air.

When all coins have been eaten by the machines, he takes you to the social club, where he drinks a pint of beer, smokes three

4711

cigarettes and plays a game of darts. You drink lemonade and eat crisps in the corner. A woman who smells of perfume, with high heels on, comes over to talk to him. He winks at her as she sits on the barstool, her legs rocking to the sound of Matt Monro playing from the jukebox overhead.

At midday, you both walk back to the house. Your grandmother is sitting in the living room with her arms crossed, staring at the carriage clock.

'What time do you call this?' she says. 'You smell of smoke. And beer.'

She stares at your grandfather with the death viper glance as he hangs up his coat, ignoring the words that spill from her mouth.

'Come on, now. We've work to do.'

On the table are pairs of Marigold gloves, cleaning cloths are folded over the chair. Pulling her tartan tabard on, she opens her bucket bag, removes copies of the Kingdom Hall's *Find Family Happiness* pamphlet, and fills up the space with cleaning products. In her eyes, cleanliness is akin to godliness. The devil hides in dirty places. Her cleaning job is important work. Before starting her shift every day, she reads passages from the Bible, then meditates on what she has just read as she scrubs the floor and buffs the windows with vinegar, hot water, and classified pages from the *Holderness Gazette*.

'Get your skates on,' she says to you. 'I've a busy schedule and you can help today.'

Then she pulls you on along the road to the lighthouse, which looms large over the town, past Aunty Mussorene's house, then the terrace where your grandmother door-knocks every Thursday morning, and onwards towards the large white building at the end of the street.

BASE NOTES

When you arrive at the lighthouse, your grandmother unlocks the door with a large antique key. Once inside, she starts rushing around like a furious bluebottle, pulls the vacuum cleaner from a hidden cupboard, then pushes it around the floor, aggressively.

'Slow down!' you say to her. But she cannot hear you for the roaring of the hoover. Standing beneath the spiral staircase, you look up towards the roof.

'I don't want to go up there. It's too high.'

'Don't be daft! You're coming up to clean with me. I need you to polish the lamp at the top.'

'But I'm frightened. Going high makes me feel poorly.'

She frowns at you, grabs hold of her sweeping brush, then grabs hold of your jumper collar with her left hand.

'Nonsense,' she laughs, with a tone that suggests you have no choice in the matter. 'Get up the stairs now, Moaning Minnie. We've a service to get to later, and I want no complaining.'

Your grandmother is walking behind you carrying her brush, which she taps on the back of your legs as you slowly start ascending towards the top, feeling sicker with each step, as the ground gets smaller below. Clinging onto the rope banister, your body goes stiff halfway up and does not let you climb any further. Your pulse is pumping faster; it feels like you are going to throw up. This is worse than being trapped in the car's back seat on a winding road.

'Grandma, I can't go any higher.'

She puts down her brush, shakes her head, and starts to laugh.

'You are such a carry-on. Always causing a fuss, aren't you?'

Clinging to the lighthouse wall, you slide down onto the stone step and try not to cry.

'When is Mum coming to get me?'

'Having a screaming abdab are we? You'll be here until the

end of summer, so you best get used to it. If you can't get up there, you can go polish the museum instead. But only the woodwork. Don't touch anything else, because if you do, I'll know and more importantly, Jehovah will know. He sees everything. If you misbehave or cause any trouble, he is watching, and believe me, he will punish you.'

'I'll just polish,' you say to her, with a tremor. 'I promise.'

As your grandmother moves past you can feel her eyes boring into you and wonder if she has a special eye like your mother's, which is hidden in the back of her skull. The special eye knows if you are lying, or if you have done anything wrong, just like Jehovah. It is something you live in fear of.

Edging down the stairs, you listen to her steps echoing slowly from the top, until you can no longer hear her footsteps and know, for a few minutes at least, you will be free.

Past the counter, in the next room, is a wooden box display with photographs of fishermen from the olden days, and maps of nearby villages washed away by the sea. Pulling up your socks, you zip up your baseball jacket, as you amble through the museum, into the back room.

The museum is dedicated to a film star who lived along the road when she was younger. You think about her as you spray polish onto the wooden rails, staring through the glass where a mannequin is dressed in a white feather shawl, alongside a cardboard cut-out of her husband, who she was married to before she died from leukaemia. A twinkling curtain hangs on the wall, and a make-up mirror with light bulbs around the side. There are pictures of her in Hollywood movies, and some of the furniture from her childhood bedroom.

Touching the dusty pink satin bedspread, you lean over to stroke one of her fur coats draped over a chaise longue. The room is deadly silent, so you lift the coat up, push your arms into the garment, and try on the fox fur in front of her dressing mirror. It emits the dank fragrance of musty mothballs and almost makes you sneeze. Then you try on her necklace made from green and gold, which is artfully placed over the jewellery box. There is no sign of your grandmother, so you lie down on the bed, kicking your legs in the air, and blow a kiss to yourself like the photographs, imagining you are in a movie for just a minute.

If you close your eyes and make a wish, perhaps you will make it all the way to America one day, escaping to a land of sunshine and sparkles. For a moment, you are lost in a Hollywood dream, that is until you hear footsteps in the doorway, and a loud voice booming at you from behind.

'What on earth are you doing?!' your grandmother shouts. 'Get off that bed. Now!'

Jumping up from the mattress, you pull the necklace off, as she leans over, drags the coat from your back, and says, 'This is the last time you are coming to work with me! Just wait until I tell your mother what you've done!'

A look of fear fills your face as you notice the two muddy trainer marks left on the bedspread where you have recently sprawled. For a moment, you ask Jehovah that, if he's listening, will he let you off the hook this time, so that nobody, especially your grandmother, will notice what you've left behind.

At dinner, which for you consists of the punishment of warmed-up grey porridge that you refused to eat at breakfast, you are instructed to leave the table early and put on your burgundy patent shoes.

'You look real bonny in them,' your grandmother says, as she rives your hair into bunches so tight that your scalp feels like it's about to peel off. Silently, you lean over and fasten the buckles.

4711

'Don't be rough with her,' your grandfather says. 'She's only a bairn.'

'If they don't learn discipline now, they never will,' she replies with a sadistic tone that almost suggests a level of pleasure in your muted obedience.

Grabbing your hand, she beckons you towards the door and together you walk along the road where a queue is waiting outside the Kingdom Hall in anticipation. Your grandmother is already enthused about what is going to be said. Her hair has been freshly combed out.

Before leaving the house, she squirted 4711 on her wrists three times to mask the odour of Jeyes Fluid, which she had used to mop the lighthouse steps with. She has never had a sense of smell, and has been wearing this lemon and rose perfume, which she buys from Woolworths, since the 1950s. On her feet is a pair of sensible court shoes, a wool suit with a thick navy belt and a matching handbag. Beneath one arm is a copy of the *New World Translation of the Holy Scriptures*, revised in 1961, with a dark red leather cover she polishes before each meeting. Its pages are like tracing paper, with gold on the edges reflecting like a long-lost treasure. She is walking brusquely as she waves at the rest of the congregation who are gathering outside.

'Slow down!' you shout to her. 'I can't keep up!'

Taking giant strides towards the line of parked cars, she says, 'Stop dawdling! We can't be late for this.'

Running after her in your shiny shoes and frilly cotton dress, marauding seagulls screech in the sky overhead. You ask, 'Why can't I stay with Gramps?'

'Because he's doing organ class, and you'll put him off, that's why. And besides, the meeting will do you good. Hopefully they'll mention something about obedience, which is something you need to learn.'

BASE NOTES

As you are introduced to the youths lined up outside, you start imagining the sound that will be coming from your grandfather's organ. He has been learning to play for as long as you can remember, but never seems to improve. His playing is so bad that you sit outside in the garden whenever he starts. Especially his version of 'Moon River', which he always plays and sings along to like Les Dawson performing his drunk piano routine. His singing is even worse than his organ playing, but you are forbidden from saying anything, because your mother told you that saying what you think will upset him. What you have to do is smile and say how good it sounds. Right now, you are smiling at all the people wearing beige clothes with glazed expressions who are filing into the building, pretending you are interested in what they have to say.

Everyone in your family calls going to the Kingdom Hall 'Jedderising', and this is also a word you must never mention. According to your mother, anyone who is a Jehovah's Witness is a Jedder, and if you have joined the Kingdom Hall then you have been Jedderised. You aren't allowed to tell your grandmother this is its name, otherwise she will think you are making fun of her, and that means she will take it out on your grandfather, who suffers enough already.

As you walk up the steps, she points up at the walls, telling you how your grandfather built them with his own hands, at her request.

'It is something I will always be grateful for, giving us a place of worship,' she says, as you walk into the main room, and sit quietly, before standing when the minister enters the room.

Before he begins the sermon, she leans over to you. 'And remember what I said before. Don't say anything *at all*. Stay quiet and listen. If you start playing up, I'll have to send you out.'

4711

On each chair is a copy of the latest edition of the magazine, which your grandmother has a large collection of at home. Inside are pictures of Paradise, which is where all the Jedders would like to go after Armageddon happens.

With an accent that draws out the long vowels of East Riding, the portly minister in a too-tight shirt with damp sweat rings under each armpit starts talking, 'This evening we are gathered to consider the role of preaching, how we are a line of the faithful that began with Abel and continues in spreading the good news. We are not primarily Christ's witnesses, but Jehovah's. The funds which are raised within the congregation are used to promote pioneering activity. Let us turn to Philippians 4:15–16. "At the start of declaring the good news, when I departed from Macedonia, not a congregation took a share with me in the matter of giving and receiving, except *you* alone . . ."'

For the next forty minutes, you tune in and out, instead focusing on the pictures inside the magazine on your lap which you flick through, quietly. There is a lion lying down with a lamb, and children from different countries holding hands dressed in white robes. You stare closely at a rainbow on the next page, and green fields, clear rivers filled with fish and a couple walking towards a light in the sky. You wonder if you are seeing things when you look twice at the bushes in the background. But you are sure you are not. Whoever drew this picture has been hiding rude things inside the drawing. You will not tell anyone what you have seen, but sitting here right now, you are trying to stifle a laugh. Your grandmother might chase you with the cherry tree branch if she finds out. You must not be the only child in this room to have spotted it.

Behind the lectern, the minister finishes his reading, then your grandmother is commended for her extra special effort in preaching to the coastguard on Spurn Point.

BASE NOTES

'Our sister did not manage to convert any of the worldly folk,' the minister says, 'but Jehovah God will reward her for the effort. We know she walked eight miles in the rain on her mission. This is admirable.'

There is a quiet round of applause as other members of the congregation nod at her. Your grandmother is convinced that if she tries hard enough, she will be one of the 144,000 let into the Kingdom of Heaven.

On your way home, there is a noticeable difference in your grandmother's mood, a serenity has overtaken her since the service; a more tolerant tone is in her speech.

'That was exactly what I needed today,' she says, as you both walk slowly up the road, away from the setting sun. 'Did you enjoy it?'

'I didn't understand what everyone was talking about.'

'One day you will. Sometimes you've to sit quiet and listen to what the adults say. You might learn a thing or two.'

On the front doorsteps, empty milk bottles are lined up for collection, and start to clatter as the wind picks up speed, blowing south-westerly from the continent.

'Why do you pray, Grandma?'

'Because him up there, Jehovah, he loves me, even when nobody else does. Going to Kingdom Hall makes me feel better about myself and gives me some hope. That's why I pray. And although there are lots of things we don't do, like voting, or going to war, or Christmas, or birthdays, or taking blood, what matters is that we all know Jehovah will save us on Judgement Day. And the thought of that keeps me going. Life is easier, knowing what the end will be.'

'Will I be saved on Judgement Day?'

'Not unless you're baptised into the congregation,' she replies.

'What will happen to me, then?'

She pauses for a moment, before pulling a Murray Mint from her handbag, and slips it into her mouth.

'You'll return to the earth, like everyone else.'

For a moment you start to think of your body decomposing in the ground. It doesn't sound like such a bad idea. After all, that's what graveyards are.

'If you're in the ground too, then what happens?'

'Jehovah will bring me back, raising my body from the soil.'

'What, like a zombie?'

Your grandmother starts to groan, then shakes her head.

'You've been watching too much late-night television young lady; it puts daft ideas in your head.'

GIORGIO BEVERLY HILLS

Giorgio of Beverly Hills

Porsche and Ferrari on Rodeo Drive. A bath of champagne. Krantz, Collins, Cooper. Thatcher and Reagan. Glamour, independence. Pygmalion girl. The art of provocation. Alexis Carrington. A shag pile carpet. No knickers, fur coat. Black coffee for breakfast. Luxury goods on American Express. A woman drenched down with the smell of success...

There is rising anticipation in the ballroom today. Tables are lined across the parquet dancefloor. Blow-dryers, roller brushes and tall cans of lacquer are stacked by each chair. A haze of Silk Cut cigarette smoke and Giorgio Beverly Hills hangs over the room.

Bergamot . . . green notes . . . orange blossom . . . tuberose . . . gardenia . . . orchid . . . vanilla and musk . . . amber . . . moss . . . A splash of cedarwood . . . You can taste that perfume on the tip of your tongue. It is the overpowering fog from your mother's salon; when you sweep up hair or wash dirty scalps in the sink, it is the one that sticks in your throat. Giorgio is the unofficial perfume of this profession, one that radiates from scented strips glued inside the pages of fashion magazines on every reception area, including your mother's salon, Reflections. Each apprentice wears the scent like a badge of pride. It is a fragrance that shouts ambition and success: the two things that matter most in life, according to the adverts.

From the corner of your eye, you can see your mother. She is waiting to sashay onto the competition floor with her model, Margot, a young woman with platinum blonde hair and layers of heavy make-up. Beneath her cutting cape is an ornate dress, off-the-shoulder, that cost over £200. Her body is tiny, her waist 24 inches. Many late nights are spent practising with Margot, who resembles a porcelain doll.

Gliding her brush over the damp hair combed back from Margot's delicate features, your mother pauses. They look into each other's eyes and start to laugh at their latest in-joke. On-stage, a man wearing a cummerbund announces the competition entrants, and they all walk together towards their chairs as Madonna's 'Who's That Girl' booms from above. Your belly turns to butterflies as the 3-2-1 countdown begins.

*

Unlike many mothers, raising children and being a good wife are not the most important things in her life, which is why your sister was bundled off to a childminder as soon as your mother's Caesarean stitches healed, so she could return to work. The last thing she ever wanted was to sit at home all day, watching *Pebble Mill* and getting depressed like the housewives whose hair she cuts and blow-dries. Baking buns and cleaning the house is for others, not her. In your kitchen is a picture frame with a painting of a broken sofa, a discarded feather duster and dirty pots on the rug that says, 'Dull Women have Immaculate Houses'. A matching one on the far end of the wall reads, 'Life Is Uncertain, Eat Desserts First'.

During the week she works late in the salon, chasing her ambitions and practising for competitions. Some of her clients are wealthy and own detached houses in nearby villages; they give her large tips which they tuck beneath their ashtrays after the hairspray dries. She spends their tip money on fast cars, Droopy & Browns dresses, gold jewellery and sending you to afterschool clubs: St John Badger Brigade, Brownies, Water Babies, Young Farmers, but never the youth club. You are forbidden from going there in case you get caught up with those from the wrong end of town. She is worried you'll start smoking and taking drugs, and roam around the estate on stolen bikes, just like they do.

By sending you to elocution classes your mother hopes you will learn to talk like a lady on the BBC, unlike the rest of the children in your neighbourhood. She doesn't want you to be 'a pleb, like everyone else', she wants you to be the best, to speak better than her, not to fail. In order to achieve this, you are sent to Alison Lee's Academy of Drama & Dance. Hopeless at choreography, you have at least mastered the art of enunciation and recounting lines by heart. All your natural shyness and introverted nature is ironed out. Although it isn't your real one, you have learnt how to put on a face.

To get anywhere in life, your mother believes it is essential to learn how to behave around those of a higher class. If you are going to meet a prince, then you must talk like a lady, or so she keeps telling you. When in fact, you'd rather just be yourself. Not the version your mother expects you to be. Right now, it feels like you have no choice about the person you are allowed to become.

*

A parade of gleaming chandeliers hangs from the ceiling, small faces peer down from the balcony above as you wave to one of them from below. You are the lost children of hairdressing, those who wander between towns and cities on the 'circuit', watching your parents compete against each other. What makes you stand out are your garish shell suits, hi-top trainers, lopsided haircuts and the tinny sounds bleeding from your Walkman headphones.

On Sundays you are driven to crumbling ballrooms, nightclubs and racecourses around the country – then you are expected to entertain yourselves until the results are announced seven hours later. Some days it feels like the most tedious way to spend an afternoon. Unless you come home with a trophy in the boot, that is. Recently, the mahogany cabinet has started filling up with silverware and rosettes at home. Your mother's dedication is finally paying off.

Staring up from the ballroom towards the stage where a

BASE NOTES

large cup is placed on a table, you spy a trophy that your mother already believes has her name engraved on it. It is the British Hairdressing Championship, a prize she has been chasing for as long as you can remember. Now it is 1988, she is ready to bring the silverware home, back over the Pennines, to Reflections, the epicentre of her existence.

*

Most of your mother's evenings are spent crafting small hairpieces with diamantés threaded through them. Made from human hair, they are designed to look like shells washed up on a tropical beach. Before bed, you often watch her work from the other side of the living room as she hunches over a polystyrene head for hours at a time, attaching long measures of hair from a seam on the crown with brass pins gripped between her teeth. She then brushes the hair out, back-combs it, and starts again until the hair contains enough glue to stand up on its own. Using her large hands and long fingers (which are the size of a grown man's, just like her size 9 feet), she moulds the hair into a shape, then threads tiny jewels into a coil, leading down the centre of the piece, like a precious ornament bought from Fenwick's on a polished mantelpiece.

*

Spraying a halo of shine mist around Margot's head, your mother coughs three times, then pulls her gown from her delicate shoulders. There is one minute before time is called in the ballroom and the stylists must leave the models. She is pleased with her evening wear look and takes a deep breath before brushing stray hairs from her dress. Rolling up her brushes into a bag, she unplugs the tongs, and places Margot into position, as if she were a mannequin in a department store window. The tables are cleared away, and she walks over to find you with a look of glee slapped across her face.

The judges walk out onto the floor as the MC announces their names, which includes the editor of *Hairdressers Journal*. The editor is very loud and very posh. He wears tight black leather trousers; it looks like a cucumber has been shoved down the front of his pants. 'Just look at the size of that,' you hear people say. Each one of the judges has a clipboard and starts to circle the models. You ask when the fantasy competition begins. That is the only competition you get excited about.

'Quiet!' your mother says. 'Can't you see, they're all circling Margot. They keep slowing down . . .'

In the next room, the models are dressed and having their final make-up touches applied for the fantasy category, which is the penultimate competition of the day. You can see Frankenstein's bride, a man dressed as Pegasus with cardboard wings and hooves, and a Mos Eisley-themed woman with gold fingernails, and a hairpiece that resembles a giant chimney brush.

Lacing up your trainers, you shake the chicken-in-a-basket breadcrumbs from your lilac tracksuit, the latest version from Dash. Its colour makes your olive skin turn grey, but you insist on wearing it, even if it doesn't suit you. Mandy, one of the salon girls, smirks and says you look like a boy in this outfit, especially with your new haircut. Your mother gives you a hug, and tells you to take no notice, that teasing is part of life. It's something you'll have to get used to.

The current hair trend at school is the 'Daphne' style, which is a short chrysanthemum fringe, and a long drape at the back, inspired by a character in *Neighbours*. Seeing as it's the Easter holiday, you have rubbed in a chestnut colour mousse which has started to drip down the side of your face in the ballroom heat. You are not old enough to wear make-up yet and distract attention from your nose, which has only just popped out and is twice the size of anybody else's your age. At school, the boys have started running past you pretending to be aeroplanes, joking about the size of it.

'Don't get upset,' your mother keeps saying. 'Your face will grow into it. I think you look a bit like that Baby Houseman in *Dirty Dancing* . . . no one puts Baby in the corner!'

Already you have started thinking about plastic surgery, especially since falling from a tightrope at Lightwater Valley last year, and straight into a sandpit, with no sand. Since then, you have been in and out of the doctor's surgery, having your nose cauterised with a soldering iron as it keeps bleeding at least three times a week, and now has a lump halfway along the bridge. Until it heals, the doctor says you might not smell anything at all, anything aside from Giorgio Beverly Hills, that is.

*

The sound of your mother's salon is one of fake sympathy, neighbourhood scandal, and the low hum of overhead dryers. It is here that you learn to listen in on conversations, hearing all about the private lives and outrageous behaviour of the Mrs-next-doors, the tragic deaths, or gleeful gloating of those who thought they were something but have now lost everything.

Asking subtle questions, your mother is almost like a therapist to the women who visit her for 'cul-de-sac' cuts in the fashion of Princess Diana. The salon is not really about clients having their hair done at all, it's about feeling better when they leave. Like her, you listen with care when clients talk to you, stop yourself interrupting, and sit with them until their rollers are brushed out, or their hair is 'done', and they are ready to face the world. Some recount stories of growing up in mill-owning dynasties, the brewing aristocracy, or speak of their childhood as daughters of stockbrokers and lawyers. They tell you about their fears and obsessions, what irritates and upsets them, but also about art, theatre and opera, a world you have never experienced but are curious to discover.

Eavesdropping on adult conversations has become your greatest asset, listening in a skill you excel at. Working in the salon, you overhear dreadful things that children aren't meant to know and then repeat them back to your friends at lunchtime, where you all sit together in a circle on the school playing field, telling tales about each other's families to make each other laugh. Keeping quiet is the key to finding out all the secrets. Already, you know far more than you should.

*

After the fantasy competition ends, you sit by the dancefloor with Big Willie MacKenzie who starts talking to you. He is your mother's trainer in the British team, together they compete in the Olympics of hairdressing. They are currently working on the next stage of her competition career, Amsterdam's Golden Tulip. To have a fighting chance at winning, she must spend at least five nights a week in the salon after work. Dedication and practice will pay dividends, according to Willie, who is not only a respected hairdresser in Glasgow, but a champion wrestler too.

His presence is so large it fills the room. He has a long handlebar moustache, soulful eyes the colour of crow's feathers, and thick bushy eyebrows. His physique is stout like a coal hod carrier. When he isn't wearing his work clothes, he likes wearing leather braces and biker boots. He jokes that he is 'a big black bear ready to take on the world'.

At Christmas he always sends a naughty card which your mother hides at the top of her wardrobe. If you pull a chair out and balance three cushions on it, you can reach the box of things she tries to hide. His cards often have a naked Santa on the front, with a miniature hat and beard balanced on the end of his you-know-what. In the staffroom, by the tint-mixing stand, a Chippendales calendar is hung on the wall, which he sent her too. All the male models wear a bow tie, and have muscles like oily balloons, no chest hair, bulging pants, orange suntans and white teeth. They are not like any men you have seen before, but looking at the calendar has become a running joke between the salon girls who keep screaming with laughter each time they flick through its pages. Thongs are not the sort of underwear that men wear in your town, your mother says it is more of 'a Y-front place', although Willie insists they are popular on the wrestling circuit.

The last time Willie came to stay on a training weekend, he told you that he shuts his salon early and goes out drinking every Thursday with Marti Pellow from Wet Wet Wet. This is incredibly glamorous in your mind, and even more so in your mother's. Marti Pellow is one of her serious celebrity crushes, although not quite on the scale of Bruce Springsteen, the man who she believes was made for her.

*

Chasing the competition dream is a way of your mother avoiding being at home. Your parents proudly describe themselves as *workaholics* and live separate lives. She jokes to her customers that her husband has 200 females that are far more important than her, they just happen to be of the Friesian variety. Except you know that it isn't really a joke, that inside she is upset at the lack of attention.

For him, the farm always comes first. The cows take up all your father's days and fill most of his weekends. For the past two years he has forgotten to buy her a Christmas present. He leaves for work at 5 a.m. and doesn't return home until after tea. In the early hours he is often called out to attend to the animals. He always smells of silage and slurry: his hair, his skin, his clothes. Your mother recoils when he tries to put his arm around her. You have started to notice how different they are. It is puzzling why they stay together at all.

*

After the fantasy competition ends, there is a long break, then speeches, with the results announced at 7 p.m. You have been hanging around since midday and still have two hours to wait. The hairdressers are ordering vodka, lime and sodas at the bar, the bubbling sound of drunken anticipation rises in the air.

In the corner of the bar is your mother, who is exhausted after styling two competitions today. She is surrounded by her junior staff's models who have unlit cigarettes hanging from their mouths. Their hair is cut into severe wedges, with undercuts and rooster feathers on top. Most are five shades of red.

'Mum,' you ask. 'Can I go outside to see the sea?'

'Well . . . don't be gone too long. Are you wearing your watch?'

'Yes,' you sigh, annoyed by her nagging, as you hold out your left wrist with a fake neon Swatch.

Then she is pulled away by her teammates, who start talking to her beneath the bar's swirly ceiling. You wave, she gestures back, and you run out towards the foyer, past the shopping centre

BASE NOTES

and head towards the Tower, which is looming above, overlooking the sea.

Overhead there are signs for the Pleasure Beach, a place your friends talk about at school. It can't be far, you say to yourself, so you start walking along the Golden Mile as the bright April sun beats down on the pavement. Trams roll past as you walk at speed, and you pass Coral Island, which is just like Muggies, and shops selling kiss-me-quick hats, buckets and spades and rude seaside postcards with drawings of puny men and overweight wives, cheating husbands, large bosoms and naughty nurses which you stop and stare at in bemusement.

By the time you reach the Pleasure Beach gates at the far end of the promenade, the light is already starting to fade. A fog of fried onion smoke floats along the road. You buy a small bag of hot doughnuts, then tokens from a hatch and start wandering around the rides with music and sirens blasting into the air. There is a log flume, a rattling rollercoaster which looks like it might collapse, a hall of mirrors, and the ride you have walked all this way for, the Haunted Swing.

Joining a queue, you wait at the railings to be called inside the door. A line of excitable children and their parents are waiting to enter. You follow them and sit inside a room with two benches. The walls are painted as if you are sitting in a Victorian living room. There is a window looking out to a green garden and a lampshade on the floor. The door closes and everyone laughs. Parents and old people are in here, too. You can hear them saying how they used to come to this ride years ago, that Blackpool is famous for it.

Classical music starts to play, then a loud creaking noise, and then the room starts turning upside down. Slowly at first, as if you don't notice it, and then much faster, with ghostly sounds around you.

'I feel sick,' a child wails.

'It's like I've had three pints too many,' a man says.

Another replies, 'Like when you have to stick your leg out the bed after drinking too much.'

The adults find it side-splitting, but you are dizzy and can sense the doughnuts turning somersaults in your stomach. The room is upside down, but it feels like you are upside down on the bench.

'Please make it stop!' you yell. 'I'm not feeling very well. Let me out.'

A woman sitting beside you grabs you by the arm and leans towards your ear. 'The trick is to close your eyes, then it'll go away. It's an optical illusion. If you were really upside down, your hair would be hanging above your head.'

You do as she says and immediately the sickness stops. And for the next few minutes you listen to the screams and cries on the benches surrounding you and concentrate on the seat, which you now know is not moving at all, then stroke the locks of your Daphne mullet, which are resting on your jacket shoulders.

When you leave the ride, it is almost dark. Wandering up to the exit, you walk onto the street and look at your watch. It is 6.40 already. You are late and need to return to the ballroom, which is a long way back up the promenade. A ripple of fear rushes through your body as you realise time has run away from you.

Jogging erratically along the seafront, waves foam over the railings as the tide crashes onto the shore. By now, you are overwhelmed with panic and keep stopping to catch your breath, before sprinting again for as long as you can manage. Fairground signs flash past, and when you finally reach the Tower, there is a painful stitch in your diaphragm. Ahead of the shopping arcade, at the entrance to the Winter Gardens, you can see Mandy, your mother's apprentice, who is pacing about the street.

'Where the hell have you been?' she shouts as the wind catches her over-bleached hair, blowing it into her face as you head towards her. 'Your mum's going apeshit looking for you.'

'Sorry,' you cough, struggling to breathe. 'I . . . I . . . I went to the Haunted Swing. I didn't know how far it was.'

'I can't even tell you how much trouble you're in.'

Dragging you back into the ballroom, she points to where your mother is sitting, with her head in her hands, and Willie consoling her. You can tell she is livid from the colour of her neck.

'Look what the cat dragged in,' Mandy says, with a smirk across her face. 'I found her outside.'

Standing up in fury, your mother pulls you towards her bosom, and makes a familiar angry-upset noise from her chest. 'We were going to call the police. *Everyone* has been out searching for you. In the rain! Just what the hell have you been doing?'

'Erm . . . I went to the Pleasure Beach . . .'

'What?! That's miles away.'

'I didn't know how far it was. Then . . . It was dark outside, so I came straight back. I'm sorry.'

She shakes her head and frowns. 'You didn't tell me you were going down there.'

'I did.'

'You didn't.'

'I did, Mum. You weren't listening.'

You know you are in serious trouble.

'Don't ever do that again,' she declares with a ferocious intent. 'There are horrible men out there, do you hear me? You don't understand this yet. But you will. I've been going spare. It's the last time I bring you to anything like this. The last time you ever come to a competition. We. Are. Through.'

*

Although you do not know what you will be when you grow up, one thing you are certain of is not becoming a hairdresser. Styling hair is the family profession. An uncle was famous for cutting and blow-drying Jimmy Savile's bouffant in the 1960s, your great-grandfather who had his legs blown off in the trenches was known in Hull as 'the legless barber', and even your aunt was a hairdresser for a while. But now it's just your mother carrying on the tradition.

Sometimes you see her perming hair and watch the outline of her body in the mirror's reflection; it is far bigger than anybody else's you know. When she stands on the bathroom scales at home or is forced to return clothes bought off the peg, she often bursts into tears. When she is upset, she eats a whole packet of biscuits in one go. After two weeks at keep fit she gave up as it injured her back. Instead of wearing spandex and legwarmers, she decided to go on a milkshake diet after getting stuck between the car door and the garage. 'I've enrolled at fat class, this time it's serious,' she keeps telling you. That's why there are only Lean Cuisines in the freezer and Ryvita in the cupboard at home. Being thin, according to your mother, is the key to achieving your dreams.

People in town call her 'Big Angie': it is a name that hurts her. Your father always says he likes her just as she is, that he doesn't care about her having 'a large pair of milkers', things like that don't matter to him. But it matters to her. Once she told you that although she laughs when people make fun of her, it is really an act. She despises the body she was born with, and wishes she had skinny genes, just like the models she likes to look at in all the fashion magazines. One thing is for certain, even if her clothes don't fit, at least her dressing table is full of expensive perfumes that make her feel better about herself. Smelling nice doesn't depend on how many custard creams she has eaten. This is a fact she is grateful for.

*

You are sitting cross-legged in a long corridor that leads down to the stalls. The Empress Ballroom's carpet is carnelian and cream, with brass fittings.

'Are you OK?' Willie asks as you dab your wet forehead with a paper tissue.

'No. I think so. Yes. I don't know. I'm tired.'

Bending down to sit next to you he says, 'It's fine to get frustrated with your mum, happens to us all. Even when we get old. Mine's eighty and we still wind each other up.'

'I wasn't doing it to upset her,' you say. 'I just wanted to go out by myself. I'm old enough now. Nothing happened.'

'Hey, it's a big day for her, so your mother's stressed. You know what she's like, blows her top and says what she needs to say, then forgets about it an hour later. I work with her, so she's the same with me. And everyone else she works with.'

Rolling the tissue into a ball in your hand, you start to smile. At least you're not the only one on the receiving end.

'Dad says she has a short fuse. That she's a bull in a china shop.'

Rolling his head back, Willie lets out a loud laugh. 'He's not far wrong there.'

For a few minutes he asks about your dad, who he has a soft spot for. 'You know, the last time I saw him, we went out drinking . . . but we'd been for a Chinese and hit the saké wine first . . .

then your father took me round all the pubs and bars, and some of the guys started having a go at me when they found out I was gay, you know? They were doing Kenny Everett impressions, flipping their hands over at me, as if I was buttoned up the back. But then he told them about my wrestling medals and the black belt I've got. They soon shut up after that. By the end of the night, they were buying me drinks. But I still could sink more than them. As we left that pub, the Bay Horse, I remember one of them said to me, "You're not bad for a poof." I must have passed their test, what an honour, eh?'

'He always goes on about how you drank Mum's royal Bell's whisky when you got home, even her Prince Harry christening bottle.'

Willie nods his head in agreement. 'Aye, we were steamin'. I won't ever forget that night. We drank until the sun came up. He's a good man, your father.'

Taking you by the hand, he pulls you up onto your feet, puts his thick wrestler's arm around you and kisses the top of your head.

'Before you know it, you'll have flown the nest. Only a few more years of putting up with each other now. Patience, patience . . .'

*

Winning is important to your mother. Every time you drive to a hairdressing competition, she taps on her steering wheel and talks to herself. Words like 'today will be my big day', or 'what matters most is the effort'. After winning, driving is her second favourite hobby.

When she drives along the road at night, you feel safe sitting alongside her, even when she's singing Meatloaf out of tune and not watching the dual carriageway properly. She wears driving gloves and takes each manoeuvre seriously. In the seventies she was named Young Driver of the Year in the *Hull Daily Mail* and managed to beat her brother in the competition, a fact she often reminds you of.

They grew up in a prefab, a house so cold that the wind rolling straight off the stormy sea blew through gaps in its walls. Both were obsessed with being the best and making as much money as possible. He died in an accident after watching Hull KR play on Boxing Day. The car rolled, the driver survived, but your uncle was trapped by crushed metal and his seat belt, which he couldn't unfasten. Water from the ditch filled his lungs until he could no longer breathe. Since then, your mother has always wanted to win for him. She says it is her way of remembering.

*

Taking her inhaler out of her handbag, your mother pumps two squirts into her mouth, sucking the puffer's spray far into her lungs before breathing out slowly. No matter how much she squirts into her lungs, she can never breathe properly and always has chest infections. Behind her, Mandy and her model are huddled together on the ballroom's velvet seats.

As you start chewing a slab of Hubba Bubba which one of the hairdresser's kids had in their pocket, your mother pulls a face. She thinks it is revolting. Bubble gum, like *Grange Hill*, is top of the banned list at home. You are not allowed to chew one or watch the other, because only the wrong kind of children like them. Being young is about restrictions, but whatever she forbids is what you are most interested in doing. When she isn't looking, you chew two Hubba Bubbas at once. And Zammo, the drug addict from *Grange Hill*, is your first serious crush. Both of these things must be kept from her. Becoming a teenager is all about the art of discretion, and the ability to deceive adults, this much you know.

*

After the speeches, the clock strikes, and you watch the judges walking onto the stage as a hush descends over the audience. It has taken much deliberation, but they have come to a decision. The head of the judges, Christine Brett, totters up to the microphone. She is dressed head-to-toe in tiger print; she has tiny feet and the highest heels imaginable. 'The points are very close; it has been a very difficult decision to make,' she announces in her rich Lancashire accent, 'because of the quality and dedication we have witnessed, which is testament to all who have entered today . . .'

Willie gives your mother a hug and mutters in her ear that no matter what happens, Margot was the finest model she has ever presented, that he is proud of her and everything she has achieved.

'You were the most fabulously dressed woman out there on the floor, by a long shot,' he says. 'Absolutely radiant in that polka dot dress.'

Opening her green marble compact, she sponges powder onto her nose, listening for her name to be called from the stage. 'Thanks, Willie,' she says, her words vibrating in anticipation. 'It's the first time anyone's given me a compliment this year.'

Your mother leans over and squeezes your hand. 'This just might end up being the best day of my life after all,' she whispers.

Pausing for a moment, you look up towards her, the bouquet of red roses onstage, and the silver trophy which is being pushed into place. Chandelier lights twinkle on her face. This is her kingdom, the competition drama the only thing that nourishes her.

'What matters most is the effort,' you reply.

DEWBERRY

Body Shop

Torn tights and denim shorts. Sixteen-hole boots. Foot lotion. Fruit shampoo. Grunge and gunge. Long henna hair. Arguments/ thoughts in black and white. Saving the whale, saving the planet. Cruelty-free, rainforest aware. Shop door queues of adolescent girls. Silvery bath pearls. Radical views. Rebellious, forthright, always self-assured. Sickly scents for Generation X...

When you were small, and it was your father's turn to have you that weekend, he'd take you along to the match, calling into the club beforehand, where you'd sit in the men's bar, eat prawn cocktail crisps and listen to him shouting about league tables, scores and betting odds in mind-numbing detail. You were often the only girl there. Even then, you never understood how he could remember the weather on that day the team played in 1983, the line-up including reserves, even who the referee was. When he talked about sport at home, your mother would roll her head back and start snoring, making a noise like a grizzly bear. Then she'd tell him to stop droning on, before pouring herself another brandy from the decanter.

Five minutes before kick-off, he would slurp the dregs of his pint, and drag you towards the turnstiles, where you would stand in the same place every other week, tenth step from the bottom, and listen to the ear-splitting Tannoy announcing players as they ran, waving, onto the pitch. Sometimes he would pull you onto his shoulders, and you would watch the game from up there. You didn't understand the rules, or why the fans were getting so excited, furious or desperate. Their faces turned scarlet, and they would stamp their feet, swearing so aggressively that sometimes it frightened you. Listening to your father shouting up from between your legs, he would grip onto your feet with his strong hairy hands and tell you not to worry, it was just how men behaved at the match, and that you shouldn't get upset. Behind, at the top of the terrace was a small urinal block and a patch of grass. From shoulder height, you watched the fans run up there before half-time, and take a long steaming piss onto the ground. You remember the smell of that grass, and the smell of the men on the terrace. Unsettling, acidic, irate.

*

You are now old enough to go to the football on your own. Every other week, you walk into the ground with other fans the same age as you. Wearing scarves, hats and jackets in the club's colours, you descend onto the terraces together and return home from each regular defeat on the noisy diesel bus.

Recently, you have grown so tall all your clothes have been replaced. Five foot six is a good height, according to your mother, but it makes you stand out at school. Most of the boys are short, and some are still the size of children, but you are as tall as the fifth years already. Your body has changed; now you must wear a bra and have hair between your legs. There is even a faint moustache above your lip, which you are not sure what to do with. At school, the boys have a nickname for you. It is not a cute name, or one that makes you look enticing in the eyes of others. It is a name that officially includes you as *one of the lads*. Your new name is Desmond. With a name like Desmond you will never get a boyfriend, a fact you are certain of.

You have not kissed anyone yet but when you were washing pots at the White Horse on New Year's Eve, you drank three bottles of K cider with blackcurrant poured in, then a pig farmer's son wearing a Huddersfield RU shirt with an upturned collar pinned you to the wall outside as you tried to get some air, forcing his hot furry tongue into your mouth at midnight, before you pushed him away. Afterwards, you were sick on the expensive new carpet at home, all the way up the stairs. Your mother shouted before your father carried you to bed and cleaned up the vomit left behind. It stained the cream wallpaper purple. Your only kiss so far is a stolen one.

After the whistle blows, you sneak into the club bar. People say you look older than your age, and because you know how to talk like an adult, you can get away with being in pubs if you don't make a fuss. Digging into your purse, you pay for a fizzy drink and sit at the end of the bar behind a group of loud men, watching, listening and earwigging. The noise subsides as the team walk into the room, and the bar erupts with cheers. The players are wearing suits and are in high spirits after their victory.

'Ready for a night on the tiles?' one proclaims, before slapping his teammate on the back, almost winding him from the blow. Swinging your legs on the stool, you slurp the dregs of lemonade through a straw and watch a player down a whole pint of bitter in one go. You think about the silly girls who have recently started coming to matches to eye up the players, and what they'd make of you sitting here, now, in the same room as the team. They would be jealous, and although it's bad to think this way, it makes you glad inside. You have something they don't have; you are already in the club.

Catching your reflection in the bar till mirror, you stare at the spot on your chin that you smothered in concealer this morning. The face you once had is starting to disappear; you can see what kind of adult you might turn into. She is not the pretty woman you envisaged. Instead, she is a mix of all your ugly relatives. This version of you is disappointing, but it is one you must live with, for now.

After putting 50 pence into the jukebox and selecting three songs, you notice an older player is watching you, so you walk into the toilet cubicle, with a warm sensation in your chest and lock the door behind you. As you let the hot pee fill the pan

BASE NOTES

below, a blot of pink appears when you wipe, so you wedge seven pieces of tissue into your pants, zip up your stonewash jeans then wash your hands under the scalding tap. Your mother does not know you have started your period; you hide the blood from her whenever you can. She does not talk to you about such things. You have had to learn the facts of life on your own.

Your Tammy Girl denim jacket smells of Body Shop's Dewberry. Blackcurrant . . . grapefruit . . . red apple and pear . . . freesia . . . jasmine . . . lily and rose . . . apricot, peach . . . cedar and musk . . . And a slightly bitter stink of sweat. Once again, you forgot to put deodorant on today. This is the same odour as most of the girls at school, the same one in changing rooms, bus seats and corridors. Dewberry and sweat are everywhere right now.

    When you sit back down on the barstool, a few of the team are standing nearby. You try to think of something to say to catch their attention. Last week you read *Hollywood Wives* from your mother's Jackie Collins books concealed in her knicker drawer, and now you are trying to remember some of the lines. Being a woman is easy if you know how to talk sexy.

    For a few minutes you shuffle about in your rucksack, then pull out the match programme, clearing your throat.

    'Hey, lads,' you say. 'Good match today.'

    They turn around and smile. The players are all wearing strong aftershave and hair gel. Some have perms. On their wrists are heavy watches, bought from airports in exotic places.

    'Great save in the second half. Should have been man of the match.'

    A player sticks his chin out, rolls his shoulders, and slurps lager through his large moustache.

    'Thanks, love,' he scoffs. 'We don't normally get young lasses saying things like that to us.'

DEWBERRY

Your cheeks turn bright pink, and you hold out the programme with a biro.

'Will you sign my programme?' you ask, pushing it into his hands, fingers swollen like raw Richmond sausages.

'What's your name?' says the player.

There is an awkward silence, as he moves a little closer.

'Want a drink?'

'I'm too young.'

'Oh, don't worry about that, sweetheart, I'll sort you out. You look at least sixteen.'

'Great, then,' you reply. 'Vodka, lime and soda. With a straw.'

The next half an hour is a blur. You parrot score facts from your father's ramblings so they will all be impressed, as if you are a child genius. They start gathering around you; it is the first time you have had any attention from grown men. Then you try to flirt, like the women in late-night films on television. It isn't too hard. The player makes a roaring belly laugh at your jokes, even the one where you say, 'I can take both of you on.' And before you know it, he offers to give you a lift home in his car, despite his teammate telling him not to.

'I'm going that way anyway,' he says. 'Can drop you off. Need to pick up my suit from home . . . off out tonight. It's no trouble, you can't be catching the bus now. It's dark and you never know who's out there.'

It is almost 6.30 and you have already missed the bus. It makes sense to get into the player's car; you won't have to walk to the bus stop, and your parents won't know you've been hanging around afterwards if you arrive back on time. You smile and agree to his offer but cannot understand why the other player is pulling him back, saying 'don't do this, you're a dickhead' into his ear.

BASE NOTES

Unlike everyone else's you know, the player's car has an immaculately clean interior, with a polished walnut effect fascia and a Feu Orange air freshener that rocks from side to side, making you feel unsettled as he drives at full speed down the motorway. It feels good to be a passenger right now.

Just before the turn-off, the player changes gear, then puts his hand on your inside thigh, grabbing at it, firmly, as if he was squeezing a pigskin ball.

'We've missed the turn,' you say. 'We need to come off.'

He smirks, then says, 'Oh, I must have forgotten to indicate. Let's go back to mine first. I've summat to collect. Tell you what, I'll pick up my suit for tonight, then drop you back off. How does that sound?'

When you arrive at his bungalow, the blinds are drawn. You follow him in through the front door and walk into the living room containing a couple of old chairs, an ashtray full of stubbed-out cigars, and a television set with triple X videos balanced on top. Unopened bills gather dust by the letterbox. A wedding photograph with a shattered glass frame balances on the radiator.

As he starts boiling the kettle, you ask, 'Can I use the loo?'

'Just through there,' he booms.

Walking through the corridor you glimpse into his bedroom, with an unmade bed, takeaway boxes and posters of Page 3 girls pinned on the wall. One is posing on a beach, topless, wearing a snakeskin thong. Her skin is dark golden brown, the type of skin that nobody you know has in your town. Opposite the bedroom is the bathroom, and you close the door, lock it, and start to shake. It doesn't feel right being here. Your parents will be wondering what has happened to you. Outside, the night has closed in.

When you unlock the bathroom door, the player is waiting behind it.

DEWBERRY

'You took your time,' he says. 'What were you doing in there?'

And then he grabs you, pushes his tongue into your mouth and forces you up against the wall. It is sticky and tastes of plaque. You writhe and try to shove him away, but you are too small, too scared, and too weak to do anything about it.

'Please stop,' you cry, as you try to get his hands out of your trainer bra. 'I need to go home to my dad.'

'Thought you wanted some? Can't lead me on like that . . .'

And then he pushes you into the living room, where a small cup of tea is waiting on the table. He is wearing a white dry-cleaned suit and starts stroking his groin as he stares at you.

'You lasses are all the same,' he grunts. 'I'll break you in.'

And you sit four feet away from him on the opposite chair, trembling as you stare out through the gap in the blinds, hoping that someone will knock on the door and make it stop. Then, he asks a question as he vigorously unzips his fly, and you try not to look at what is in his hands. You shrug your shoulders, rigidly, not knowing what to do, and try to concentrate on the chipped porcelain cup spilling its contents from the rim. The milk is off, and white globules float on the top, as you try to slurp it into your mouth. Salty tears run down your face.

He drives in silence back to the town, but you refuse to tell him the street where you live. Shaking his head, he says, 'I'm sorry love. Let me give you a present.'

After pulling over, he turns off the engine, reaches over to the back seat, and pulls out a bag containing his kit from the day, pushing its contents into your hands.

'Here, have my shin pads.'

And you take the stinking pair of pads from him and put them in your rucksack as your little heart pounds up into your throat as if it is attempting to escape and run down the road.

BASE NOTES

'Bye then,' you say, quietly. 'Maybe see you at the match next week . . .'

Your father is sitting in his chair, listening to sport on the radio, when you walk through the back door. You mumble words about missing the bus and he tuts beneath his breath saying something about hanging around with lads. You run upstairs and remove your clothes, pulling out the dried bloody tissue in your pants, and throw the team scarf that reeks of the player's aftershave onto the bed. In the corner of the room is a fitted wardrobe. You tear down the team posters that were Blu-Tacked inside, putting the shin pads under a mound of clothes, hiding them deep so they can no longer be found. Downstairs, you can hear your mother's car pulling into the garage. She has been working late again.

*

Each night, as you drift into sleep, it feels like the player is there in the room, hiding behind the wardrobe doors, beneath the pile of clothes. It is as though he is a bogeyman, a spectre haunting your subconscious. At school, your behaviour changes. You become coarse and outspoken and overly sexual. It is not like you. You do not understand what is happening. Inside, deep down, in the place nobody else understands, you start to worry that he is inside of you, making you behave in this way. 'It's teenage hormones,' your parents keep saying, but you cannot tell them what it really is. At school, teachers keep asking if something is wrong at home, that your attitude is unusual, but you cannot tell them the truth either. It is a pact between you and the player. One that will not go away.

It is only after watching a film late one night that you realise what needs to be done. After your parents have gone to sleep, you crawl into the wardrobe, remove all the clothes, until you find

DEWBERRY

the shin pads, resting at the bottom, still covered in caked mud from the year before. You pull them out, then creep downstairs, grabbing a torch from the garage.

Slowly and calmly, you remove the large rockery stones in the front garden, excavating the soil with your bare hands. You pray that nobody can hear you and push the shin pads into the cavity, bury them with soil, covering the mound with stone, as you wrench at the trailing plants to seal the sepulchre in for good. For the first time in months, you breathe out. What you do not know yet is that the garden, with its twisted willow and rockery with broken soil, will feature in your dreams each night for the rest of your life. But at least, for now, the player's ghost is buried, trapped far down beneath the stones with no chance of ever seeing light.

TRÉSOR

Lancôme

The brown-eyed girl with smouldering brows. Spring's tender blossom. Tinned peaches in syrup. A gap in her teeth. European, profound. She sleeps in a nest of eglantine. An unpredictable tender touch. Running barefoot on a moonlit beach. Convertible cars on Highway 1. Eyelashes softer than butterfly wings…

Every Saturday morning you rifle through the charity shop hunting for clothes, records and paperbacks. All goods are affordable there, it is a treasure trove of discarded clutter. Collecting second-hand junk is a way of avoiding reality. Unlike what exists beyond it, your bedroom is an environment you can control. The walls are painted midnight blue, the air is scented with sandalwood incense, postcards of Andy Warhol's soup cans are pinned to the door, overcooked lava lamps bubble in each corner. Piles of books about New York in the 1960s are stacked by your crumpled bed. There are heaps of unwashed clothes, and a dusty chest of drawers, with empty deodorant canisters, used tissues and almost-spent bottles of perfumes littered on the surface.

The young woman you have become is not the variation your mother had hoped for. After much argument, and in an act of desperation, she permitted you to attend art college so you could finally 'join in with the freaks'. She is often confused by the men's suits you wear, your big boots, the unlistenable music you enjoy, the militant left-wing views you have cultivated, your belligerent attitude and general character. It is far too removed from her. The separation between you both is another problem to comprehend on top of her own marriage. The apron strings have finally been severed.

'Why can't you be more like the salon girls?' she asks. 'Bubbly and loud. Or at the very least, *normal*. Is there something wrong with you? What will my clients think? I may love you . . . but I don't have to like you.'

The only person who comes to your defence is your father, who was another square peg in a round hole. In the sixties, like

BASE NOTES

Marc Bolan, he was recruited as a John Temple Boy, with the perfect physique to model their mohair suits, which were made for sharply dressed mods. John Temple's tailors nicknamed him 'King Charles' due to his handlebar moustache and kitted him out from their Leeds store in exchange for catalogue modelling. When your father looks at your clothes, he says it reminds him of times past, and unlike your mother, he is not ashamed of the adult you are becoming.

Like most of your friends, you wear malodorous Afghan coats, knitted tank tops and platform shoes of the recently deceased. Even after washing, these antique clothes smell of the odour of others, or perhaps multiple owners. You spray Trésor under the armpits to eradicate the fug before wearing. Apricot blossom . . . lilac and rose . . . lily-of-the-valley . . . iris and jasmine . . . heliotrope . . . vanilla . . . sandalwood . . . amber . . . musk . . . A trace of bergamot . . . But no matter how much of the fragrance you spray on your clothes, the grotty underlying tang of strangers' perspiration is immovable. It is a perfume that will always remind you of this upside-down year.

You now reside in a bungalow near the graveyard, with an outdoor toilet, no central heating, leaking window frames, and the sort of carpet that makes you think you're hallucinating if you stare at it too long. After your mother left your father a few months ago, you arrived here. It is the only place she can afford after selling half her business to pay off debts. For years she had been spending everything she earned on hairdressing competitions, travelling and buying dresses for Margot, then started borrowing more to cover it up.

Before their separation, your father kept saying: 'Spend! Spend! Spend! Your mother's worse than Viv Nicholson!' He would rather save every penny and live on a pittance, eating

TRÉSOR

out-of-date toast each night in a tied house on a random farm out in the wilderness, just like the one he grew up in. Money was one of the myriad reasons why they split up.

The old house was semi-detached, with three bedrooms, a gravel conservatory roof and a long garden with a twisted willow tree. It was decorated with dado rails, tieback curtains and paisley wallpaper. Rarely satisfied with how it looked, your mother always wanted to change it: new kitchen, new carpets, new sofa, new fitted wardrobes. For a while, the local joiner was a permanent fixture, always building at her behest. You would sit and watch him craft units from wood, captivated by the process, and talk for hours as he chain-smoked then constructed fittings designed from your mother's imagination, patiently explaining how every joint fitted together.

Compared to where you lived before in a gloomy new build, the house was posh. Posh in the sense of being better than the previous house, but not posh if you compared it to the estate where all the teachers and tax collectors lived. Your mother complained that the mortgage at the posh house was unaffordable, but the financial pain inflicted was worth it. Living in a posh house felt like she had finally moved up in the world. After growing up in a prefab, a council house, then a tied house, she believed that owning her own home was the only way to have security. It was, according to her hero Mrs Thatcher, the aspirational dream, and something she believed in too. All your mother truly desired was an abundance of money, foreign holidays and a nice house where she could have summer barbecues. Material things are important to her, unlike your father, who doesn't care about any of those things at all.

Now you no longer live in the posh house, you are back to square one. Your mother has plenty of hairdressing trophies on the shelf but has lost almost everything else in the process.

BASE NOTES

*

Although you have only moved a few streets away, you don't see much of your father right now. You are frustrated with both parents and don't know how to express the uncomfortable emotions boiling inside your gut.

There is a dark cloud hanging over your family, but at least you understand why. Your sister is confused by it all. She is too young to comprehend the reasons, and this causes her anxiety. On the other hand, you know far too much about your mother's rationale. Because you are articulate, and a good listener, she treats you like her therapist. Your mother believes you are mature and have enough wisdom to advise her on what to do. The pressure of knowing her inner thoughts has become too much for you to cope with. No matter how intelligent you appear on the outside, you are still only sixteen.

Despite the change in your mood and behaviour, nobody asks how you are feeling, aside from the art tutor at college, who took you out of class, putting her arm around you when you booted a chair in a 3D lesson and started shouting at everybody. You were supposed to be discussing use of composition in Carl Andre's *Equivalent VIII* when it all erupted. She was the only one who bothered to find out what had been happening at home, and asked if there was anything she could do to help.

Your mother believes your ability to dwell on things and never let them go is holding you back, that you should stop overthinking the past and move on. But already, you cannot stop raking over all the bad events that have ever happened, and never seem to remember times of happiness. Apparently, this tendency towards rumination makes you 'morose', 'a sulker' and a 'negative thinker'.

TRÉSOR

'You should stop feeling sorry for yourself,' your mother keeps saying. 'At least you have a roof over your head. At least you aren't starving. At least you didn't grow up like me, in the Kingdom Hall, where I couldn't even fart without the Bible's approval!'

The only person who understands your current turmoil is Steven Patrick Morrissey. A giant poster of The Smiths outside Salford Lads Club is tacked above your bed, and you can't stop watching the band on a recording from their *Top of the Pops* appearance in 1984, where Morrissey opens his shirt to reveal MARRY ME scrawled across his chest in marker pen.

Every night, you practise playing Johnny Marr's guitar lines from the band's songbook on an Argos guitar with nail varnish flecked on the body. Your Smiths phase has become a bit of a running joke. This obsession is hilarious in your mother's eyes, and she keeps performing impressions of Mozzer around the house, singing 'Heaven Knows I'm Miserable Now' when you take yourself too seriously. You have started playing *Meat Is Murder* on repeat to annoy her, with the sound of cows pleading in an abattoir. She's incensed that since becoming a Smiths fan you've embraced the cause of vegetarianism. Instead of eating what she suggests – boiled vegetables with grated cheese and an egg – you've started eating Pasta 'n' Sauce from a packet each night instead. As a result, you now have seven spots on your chin, and your forehead is permanently pustulant. At least Morrissey would be proud of you, that much you know, but the other part of your life is not one you could tell him about.

*

After trying on three outfits and posing in the bedroom mirror, the hallway phone starts ringing. You walk into the back room of the bungalow and pick up the receiver; your father is on the end of the line and asks if you can give him a hand with a heifer that's in trouble. Pulling on your boots, and oversized Fred Perry jumper, you lock the door, leap over the graveyard wall and trot towards the old house. When you arrive, your father, whose hair and overalls are coated in milling dust, has already started the engine, and your uncle is in the passenger seat. He has borrowed the Land Rover from work – a battered old shell that is miraculously still running. It is rusting on the outside and has an engine loud enough to scare off the jackdaws.

Winding down the window, your father beckons to you, 'jump in . . .' and you climb into the back, among a bed of ancient newspapers, crushed hay and rolls of twine rope. A miasma from an oily pot of Swarfega hangs in the air, and slowly infiltrates your tastebuds.

'How come you're here?' you enquire from the back, as you chug down the lane towards the main road.

Frantically tuning the radio for this afternoon's football coverage, he replies, 'It'll take more than two of us.'

'What do you mean by that?' you say. 'I'm supposed to be going out tonight . . .'

Turning around, your uncle looks at you, raises his eyebrows and stares at your outfit. 'You'll be needing a change of clothes in that case,' he states, before wiping his spectacles and pushing them back up his broken nose that, in a certain kind of light, resembles a smashed-in turnip.

Your father takes a cloth handkerchief from his pocket and wipes at the large wet cavern of his left nostril, then clears his throat, spitting a greenie from the window as you head past the bend by the motorway bridge. 'It's a bad birth, love . . . 'ad a call which worried me. There's an 'eifer down, trying to calve . . . but the thing is, they're all maiden 'eifers, so I 'aven't got a clue 'ow one of 'em's pregnant . . . but Ron Pig reckons she's been

TRÉSOR

down a while . . . the calving jack's in t'back, wit' ropes . . .'

Staring at the device beneath your feet, you make a muted wince. It's not the first birth with complications you have been called in to. A few years ago, you watched a Caesarean section, and helped deliver a calf with ropes. But knowing the jack is out suggests there's a problem. When you help at the farm on weekends it's normally a mucking-out job, using shit scrapers to clean the parlour, pushing gargantuan volumes of excrement and urine into the slurry drains, feeding trembling newborns with warm milk, changing their bedding, committing rodent genocide, and training cattle to walk on a halter. The vet is only called out if your father can't treat the animal himself; after working with cows for a lifetime, he understands every nook and cranny, and can often diagnose their illness just by looking at them. He says if he'd been more disciplined in his youth then he could have been a vet. But today, he can't get a call-out, so he's having to deliver the calf himself.

In a few weeks' time the farm where he works will be sold for luxury homes. The barns, milking parlour and paddocks are being bulldozed for million-pound houses, freshly built for first division footballers or wealthy accountants. Your father is also going to lose his prize pedigree beef herd he has reared for the past ten years, his dairy cows and his favourite bull, who will be auctioned for slaughter. As he doesn't own any of the animals and only works for the owner, he has no say about the change that is about to come. Losing his cows is almost as bad as losing his family and now the two have arrived at once. According to him, 'it doesn't rain, it pours'. His head is in a very dark place. He has even shaved off his tea-strainer moustache which makes his colossal nose resemble a vulture's beak. Sleepless sepia rings surround his eyes. You have started to worry about him.

BASE NOTES

*

Beyond the grazing fields are infinite acres of oilseed rape, which are now ripening, an acidic yellow haze radiates from the horizon. Already your nose is starting to run from hay fever; it is a season that causes bloodshot eyes, sneezing through the night, asthma attacks, dermatitis and a complete loss of smell throughout the month of May. The pollen hangs low over the artesian basin that you live in, the plant's pungency a symbol of summertime misery.

Across the River Wharfe, gunshots ricochet from behind Ulleskelf. Climbing out of the van, you unlock the padlock into the pasture, as your father pulls out a tub of lubrication. The skin on his fingers is hardened and stained yellow. During each shift in the herringbone parlour, he uses a cloth dipped in iodine to clean cracked teats, preventing mastitis.

'I suspect me blood'll start turning yellow soon,' he jokes.

Walking towards a nearby hedge, your uncle spots the heifer lying in the grass. Her leg has lifted up and she is panting. 'Looks bad,' he shouts across. 'Summat's stuck. Poor thing must be in terrible pain.'

Running towards her, your father leans down and looks into her eyes, nods his head and talks softly to her. You cannot hear what he says, but in the private language of cowmen, he is trying to reassure her before what comes next.

'We 'ave to get 'er up,' he says to you. 'Grab that fence panel in t'boot. I can't calve 'er laying down. We need to make a crush.'

For the next few minutes, they try to push her up from the grass, before making a halter to drag her from her stupor. She is groaning as your father slips his hand into her to feel what's inside. 'It's dead,' he says. 'And it's a bloody big 'un. I can feel its 'ead.'

TRÉSOR

Leaning against the crush fence, you keep her upright, as your father ties ropes onto the little calf hooves, connecting them to the jack, which he pushes into the soil with his wellington boot behind her.

'How did this happen?' you ask. 'She's only slight, look at her . . .'

Your father lets out a sigh and stares out across the other maiden heifers in the field. 'They've all been served,' he spits, 'by a friggin' continental. It must've swum up the river. I can feel it's a big beef breed already. That's why she can't calve it.'

He double knots the ropes, then lubricates the impossibly small hole that the calf is supposed to be pulled through, as the heifer tries to kick him from behind.

'What if we can't get it out?' you say. 'What happens then?'

Your uncle, who is still pushing against the fence crush, keeping her on her feet, starts to cough, before replying, 'Worst case scenario, we'll have to wire it. But I hope it doesn't come to that. This isn't gonna be easy, but if we don't help her, she'll die . . .'

By now, the beast's eyes are rolling, as your father gestures to take hold of the ropes and start working the jack. Leaning into her, he starts guiding the dead calf out, as you pull harder in the grim tug of war that will only end one way.

*

It is dusk. You are now sitting on the bank, watching the final rays of sun, wiping afterbirth from your hands onto the meadow grass. Overhead, skylarks weave through the oak trees, into shady woods, before dipping into deep meadows, above marshy plains of transparent floods.

Beside you, the body of a large calf is laid out, its coat covered in dry white matter, its nose congealed with blood. When you finally dragged it out of her, the heifer fell into shock, and appeared to die for a minute or two, before slowly breathing again, as your father injected her, dosing her body with enough medication to bring her back from the precipice. And now you can hear faint moaning from her, the desperate creature unaware of what has just happened. It almost sounds like the backing track to *Meat Is Murder*, only worse than Morrissey's abattoir sounds. Your father cups water into his palms and slowly drips it into her mouth, as she starts licking water from his fingers. He talks to her calmly, checking her pulse and stroking her cheeks as he shakes his head at the mess.

The sensation of wet eyeliner running down your cheek causes a tingle, and as you wipe it away with your sleeve, you notice a hole in your jeans, which must have been caused in the heave. For a few minutes, you managed to forget about your solipsism and focus on a much more important matter, which for now involves filling up a bucket of water from a trough so that your father can rinse his hands.

Behind the hawthorn hedge, you can hear your uncle peeing, before he bounds over. 'You did well today,' he says, patting you on the back. 'Showed your true colours. That wasn't an easy thing to do, and she almost died, but you kept going and that's what matters. Most girls your age would never have done that.'

You stare up at him, thinking how this is maybe the first time he's spoken to you like an adult, mumbling an awkward 'thanks' beneath your breath before walking through the long grass towards the open gate.

CK ONE

Calvin Klein

Juicy Fruit tang. Adidas Gazelles. Kurt + Kate. Her jeans unbuttoned. Still enraptured by the arrogance of youth. Mascara smudged from the night before. Pillar-box red on his chipped fingernails. Faces hot with anticipation. Heartbeats. Techno. Nicotine. Doves. Ringing ears, they chase obliteration...

The heat inside the two-man tent started just after dawn, three hours later you are lying comatose with a single duvet over your body. Tinnitus wakes you after dancing too close to the bass bin last night. Your makeshift pillow is made from a scrunched-up pair of cords wrapped in a sweater. Condensation has started to form on the nylon tent sheet, already the sun is blazing outside. You are in a field in Scotland. It is 1995.

Your friend, Charlie, is more prepared. She has brought a sleeping bag, air mattress, breakfast cans of sausage and beans, and a camping stove. Unlike you, she has been camping many times before and knows the drill. In contrast, your holdall is packed with beer, a meagre lump of hash, a feather boa, knee-high patent leather platform boots and sixteen pieces of crumbling Rimmel make-up.

As the first soundchecks begin to echo from the main stage, just along the road, Charlie starts to stir. Sitting upright, she says, 'My heaaaaad.' Her bright orange hair forms a diagonal Mohican from the static. Then she whispers, 'Water. Where's the water?'

With one eye open, you squint over at the empty Evian bottle that you finished off in the night and pretend not to notice.

She picks it up, throws it at the zip and groans, 'Fucking hell! You drank it all?'

Hauling the duvet over your head you wince a pathetic excuse from beneath, before she eventually staggers, hungover, from the tent, and walks towards the water tap in the next field, where a huge queue has already formed.

BASE NOTES

This is supposed to be your celebratory 'saying goodbye' holiday. Next month she is leaving to go to university where she is studying over in Manchester. You are frustrated, because all the interesting people live on the other side of the Pennines and the town where you live has barely any interesting people left at all. Anyone of note abandons ship as soon as the opportunity arises.

'There'll be no deviants left, except for me!' you keep saying to her. 'What am I going to do?'

You have promised to write to each other every week, and then one day, when she leaves the halls, you might rent a terrace house together in a glamorous neighbourhood, like Hulme, Cheetham Hill or Strangeways. You have already started saying it in the same way as Liam Gallagher, 'Manchestaaaaaah', with a long nasal whine.

Unlike you, Charlie is a diligent student and knows how to focus on exams. She has always been clever, but never in a way that makes you feel inadequate. Her brain is full of political and historical facts, quotes from great philosophers, and her hero, Richey Manic. Her bedroom is a shrine to him. Recently she joined Junior Labour: in times of turmoil, you both go out under the cover of darkness and flyer the streets, pushing red pamphlets through letterboxes when nobody is looking. Everyone votes Conservative in the streets where you live. You have always been the odd ones out. The resident awkward twins.

Charlie's parents live around the corner now you've moved house again. Until recently, your father was still living at the other side of the cemetery on his own, until the house sale went through. Now he's living in Wiltshire, working on a farm contract, six days a week. You know he is still upset about the divorce. He says he'll always love your mother, eternally. He can't understand why she left her life with him for the life she now has.

CK ONE

'We had the best of times,' he keeps repeating. 'A lot of fun. She did whatever she wanted.'

Yours aren't the only parents that have divorced of late, it's a contagion these days. There was no exit from doomed marriages, until recently. Many women are pleased to have shaken off their early mistakes, discarding their broken husbands as if they were spent dishcloths. Some take up with other, equally useless men, but in your mother's case, she appears to have opted for a much worse option than the last.

You now live with husband number two, who never calls you by your name. Your sister is lucky to be called by hers most of the time, but yours is simply 't'other one', which is usually chuntered under his breath whenever he is forced to speak of you. He is an awkward man who bears a striking resemblance to *The League of Gentlemen*'s shopkeeper, Tulip 'Tubbs' Tattsyrup, and enjoys all-day drinking, watching *Dad's Army* on repeat and listening to 'Video Killed the Radio Star' each time he sits behind the wheel. This has earned him a private nickname, which was invented by your sister, a little girl with the most barbaric sense of humour in town, a fact you are immensely proud of. She has decided to call him Buggles.

Since meeting Buggles, your mother has stopped wearing bright colours and is subdued. Her volume has decreased, and even though her loudness was cringeworthy, you'd rather she was herself. After leaving your father, she lost six stone on the Rosemary Conley hip & thigh diet and won 'slimmer of the year' at fat class. The diet consisted of zero fat and four slices of Ryvita and cottage cheese for lunch every day. No snacks were allowed, only starvation. Never one to miss a chance at publicity, she had her picture taken wearing a pair of size 24 jeans, holding them out to the camera with at least a foot to spare from her newly svelte body for the local paper. It is now framed and hangs above the breakfast bar as a reminder to never get flabby again.

Now your mother has a new thin person's face, but you are convinced the dramatic weight loss chipped away at her character. For a while, her neck became scraggy like a turkey's, deep lines appeared around her glistening eyes. One night she decided to go out to *show off her figure* and that's when she bumped into Buggles, who she thought, correctly, could be incredibly funny once you broke through his shyness. What she had not anticipated were his suffocating mood swings and general irritation at the children she had borne to her previous husband. He wanted her all to himself.

Instead of staying at home, where you mostly feel uncomfortable from your stepfather's monumental sulks and silences, you walk around town with Charlie at night. Together, you stare up at the stars from the top of the hill, looking down at the winking motorway lights in the distance, and dream about the future, talk about boys and bands that you like. For you, Suede are the current obsession. For her, there is no band greater than New York Dolls.

You have been friends since nursery school. The best part of knowing someone for so long is that you can be your own, raw, awful self with each other. And if you are being annoying, selfish or boastful – the other will quickly point it out.

Sometimes you irritate each other, especially when hungover or coming down from pink champagne speed, and today at the festival that is obvious.

'Did you bring paracetamol?' she asks, rolling back onto her deflating blow-up mattress. 'It was on the list . . .'

You pause for a moment, then remember a packet in your bag. 'Yes. Here.'

CK ONE

You fish out the packet, your rancid morning breath filling the tent, and dig into the box. There is only one tablet left in the foil.

'Oh, fuck. Must have forgotten to check.'

Charlie lets out a long sigh, one of the disappointed ones you know too well. It is the sigh of you being selfish again. Most of your female friends end up making that familiar exasperated sound in the end. You are never quite good enough to meet their standards. The trouble is, you haven't worked out what the invisible rules of friendship are, because you'd rather be on your own most of the time. As a child, you liked nothing more than being left to your own devices, creating scenarios in the Sindy house, reading Brothers Grimm fairy tales or listening to records with a pair of headphones on. It rarely involved anybody else. Girls at school were mostly irritating, and the boys were mostly violent, but at least they weren't two-faced. If they despised you, at least they said so. Charlie is the only friend who could ever really put up with you, but you fear her patience is wearing thin.

'Shall we buy some more painkillers and get food?' you say to her, as she wriggles into a pair of faded blue Wrangler flares, yanking them up to her waist, avoiding the recent piercing in her belly button that is turning green-gluey and septic. 'There's a service station just down the motorway. I'll buy you two packets to say sorry. And a cheeseburger for Sunday lunch.'

'You're forgiven,' she grumbles, 'just this once.'

Slavering suntan lotion all over her face and arms, her alabaster skin is covered in a filigree of freckles. There are traces of pink glitter around her eyes from last night's unsuitable glam rock outfits, a homage to your fashion obsessions: Roxy Music, Sweet and Sparks. Even the inside of the tent is twinkling.

Rather than the hygienic option of queuing for a shower, you opt for a roll-on deodorant and two fruity squirts of CK One, which is an essential you would never neglect to remember.

BASE NOTES

Lemon . . . mandarin . . . cardamom . . . papaya . . . orris root . . . freesia . . . violet and nutmeg . . . cedar, green tea . . . amber . . . oakmoss . . . pineapple, pepper . . . a hint of musk . . . You spray two squirts on Charlie, then brush your teeth from a cup outside the tent.

Together, you walk in the baking heat, through the Fata Morgana of the motorway, following the steady stream of bedraggled festival goers, towards the service station oasis. Condensation appears on Charlie's glasses when you finally reach the turn-off. She keeps removing them, wiping and replacing, before redoing the process again every five minutes. Vehicles whip past on the way in, one contains a Vauxhall packed with neds listening to a gabber mixtape at deafening volume. They are smoking spliffs on the forecourt.

'I quite fancy the driver,' she mutters beneath her breath. 'I know we'd have nothing in common, but he's fit, even with all that hair gel . . .'

You look over and wince at the boy, who resembles a teenage Ian Beale in a Kappa tracksuit. She has always had eccentric taste when it comes to men.

'Are you going to call your mum?' you ask.

'Yes, I promised I would. Just to tell her I'm still alive.'

'I'm not ringing mine. She won't care if I'm alive or not.'

Charlie raises her shoulders and shrugs.

'Bet she does care. It's just you that doesn't want to talk to her since that carry-on with he-who-will-not-be-mentioned.'

Joining the tail-end of the phone queue that is already stretching out of the door, you root into your bag flap for loose coins, pushing a warm and sticky Opal Fruit into your mouth that has gathered fluff inside the pocket for at least two months. You start to speak and chew.

CK ONE

'Living there, it's getting worse, Charles . . . When he comes back from work it's like the air's been sucked from the room.'

Charlie laughs. 'Well, you're not the easiest person to live with, are you?'

You are starting to feel under attack again but must concede she has a point.

'Me being difficult isn't a reason to smash all the windows in with a fence post, though, is it?'

She pauses, and carefully considers what to say before she speaks. You admire this trait, as a person with a tendency to blurt out words before thinking, as if your brain is constantly rushing to offload sentences backed up inside your head.

Pushing her glasses back into place, Charlie replies, 'Maybe you should try and move out? Leave them both to it. It's their business, not yours. There must be something about him she likes. Personality, intelligence, sex appeal . . .'

Throwing your head back, you make a wincing expression at her suggestions. 'I feel ill now. As if my hangover wasn't bad enough.

'I just thought she had more sense, that's all,' you sigh. 'She promised she wouldn't marry him and went back on her word. Now she's stuck with him. I always thought she had more sense but now I'm convinced that my mother is, in fact, an idiot.'

After a few minutes of standing, Charlie leans forward, picks up the receiver and calls home. She finishes the conversation quickly as a concerned look fills her face.

There is a bewildered expression in her eyes.

'Del, you need to ring home, now.'

Clicking the receiver down, you put 50 pence into the slot and quickly dial 0937. It is engaged, so you keep calling, wondering what drama has happened this time. Then the call connects.

BASE NOTES

'It's me,' you say, quickly. 'Charlie said I've to ring. What d'you want?'

There is a pause, then your mother says, 'Is she with you now?'

'Yeah. We're just at the service station waiting to get a breakfast burger and paracetamol.'

'Now, try not to get upset, but it's your dad . . . he's in hospital . . . it's serious...'

For a split second adrenaline flushes through your body as your mouth turns dry. Time stops ticking.

'What's happened?'

'He's had an accident. Quite a bad one.'

Immediately you fall silent and take a gulp. Tears form in the corner of your eyes.

'Wha, wha, what? He's done what?'

'Don't panic, but they've sent him to intensive care. A machine broke on the farm, and it swallowed him up . . .'

Suddenly, your brain fills with the image of your father being eaten by a combine harvester or drowning in the slurry pit.

'What kind of machine?'

The fear pumps so quickly through your veins that you barely hear what she is telling you.

'A bailer, apparently . . . It took his foot off. But it didn't get the rest of him, he pulled himself out. Then he laid out on the straw bleeding, the top of his foot was in the welly, but they managed to save it. I think they're trying to graft some of it back on.'

'How long was he there? I mean, was he screaming? Who found him?'

You start sobbing uncontrollably down the phone, as people in the queue start to stare out of sympathy. Charlie puts her arm around you for a hug.

'He was there twenty minutes. Your uncle found him after bringing the cows in. They got an air ambulance, so he's alive,

CK ONE

and he's had transfusions. But they don't know if he'll walk again. You're going to have to come home . . . We need to get you down there . . . I'm sorry . . .'

After saying goodbye, you hang up the phone and start to weep. Never have you felt so far away from home. Charlie holds your hand, takes you outside and sits next to you on the picnic bench. You are uncontrollable and have feelings of immense guilt. All your recent bad teenage behaviour flashes in front of you. The strops and arguments, the arrogance and bitterness. The vision of your father lying in the straw, begging for help keeps replaying in your head.

Wiping salty tears from your face, you try to speak through the shock, but find it hard to string any sentence together right now.

'I don't know if I'll ever see him again. What if he dies tonight?'

'Come on,' Charlie says. 'Try and stay positive. They might save him yet. In fact, I know they will. He's not going to die. Let's pack up the tent and go home.'

*

The day after, when you board at Leeds, the coach is fully booked, and a man who looks like a Hell's Angel sits down next to you. He is wearing a leather jacket, has long hair, a bandana, tattoos and a clanking pair of biker boots. The sugary sweet sweat of last night's session hovers on his breath. It must have been a long night. The man doesn't tell you his name, and you don't tell him yours, but he does say he's just been released from prison. Talking to strangers on public transport is a recent habit of yours. People tell you things you'd never expect.

The biker reveals he has been locked up in Wakefield jail,

serving a sentence for armed robbery. 'Now I can say I'm ex-Monster Mansion,' he cackles.

'Who were you in there with?' you ask, out of morbid curiosity. 'Anyone I'd have heard of?'

'Charles Bronson, he was in there. And Robert Black. A horrible fucker, and that's saying something coming from me. I've met a few in my time. You likely won't have heard of Paul Sykes, but could I tell you some stories about him. All the nonces are on a separate wing, and the serial killers. That's where the word nonce comes from you know, it started in Wakefield. It's short for "not on normal courtyard exercise". They can't let them mix. Anyway, that's all in the past now. I have to look forward. The day is young. And I'm a free man. Where are you heading?'

'Well, I'm errrr . . . going to Bath, but it's quicker by bus so I'm stuck on the long haul. Got my Walkman, sandwiches, bag of crisps, and this book which weighs more than a bag of flour. I was up at a festival in Glasgow. Then I found out my dad had been in an accident. He's working down in Wiltshire on a farm. I've to go and see him, that's why I'm travelling south. Because they don't know if he'll make it through the night.'

The man removes his sunglasses, revealing his bloodshot eyes.

'Oh, I'm very sorry to hear that.'

Pulling into a long line of slip road traffic, the bus slowly reaches a standstill. You wait for a moment, then say, 'It was quite gruesome, a bailing machine sliced his foot off. We don't know if he'll walk again . . . If he's disabled, I'll have to look after him, because there's nobody else. On top of that, we've nowhere to live. And no money, either.'

He licks his dry mouth, pulls a Lypsyl from his pocket, runs it over his lips, then stares out of the window. 'All the bad shit comes at once, doesn't it?' he says.

'Feels like that right now. I work in a petrol station, doing the early shift on weekends. And I'm almost an adult. This age, it's meant to be the best time of your life, isn't it?'

The man laughs. 'If you believe the myth, that is. It wasn't the case for me. Certainly not in Deerbolt.'

'Everything's gone wrong recently. I'll be glad when it's all over . . . I keep thinking about running away. Disappearing into thin air.'

'That's not always the answer, though,' he laughs. 'There's this daft idea that it'll solve all your problems.'

You stare at the lines on his face, and the tattoos on his neck, then ask, 'How long were you inside?'

He takes a long deep breath, and starts to smile, tapping his nails on the seat shelf.

'Fifteen years, so long enough to learn the lesson. Long enough to regret the decision. I needed money back then to pay a debt, so that seemed like a good idea at the time. I robbed a post office, then got caught on the way out. They don't look kindly on firearms . . .'

'Did you shoot anyone?'

'Just the ceiling . . . that landed me in hot water. On top of that, there was previous.'

You're not entirely sure if he's telling you the real reason why he was locked up for so long, but there is something about the biker of interest to you. His bad wisdom is appealing. If Charlie was here, she'd have a crush on him. Part of you wonders if you might have one too.

'I'm getting off at Birmingham,' he says, as the coalfields turn to suburbs, and the suburbs turn to warehouses in the landscape outside. 'Heading to the Black Country, where my new life begins.'

A hip flask is in his pocket, and he shares it with you. Trees are absent as far as the eye can see, acres of flat land fade into the distance. A starling cloud explodes from a fishing pond. The afternoon sun sets in the west.

You reach into your jacket and pop a tablet into your hand, before swigging it down with a hit of his lukewarm bourbon.

'Mother's little helpers?'

'They don't seem to be working very well,' you remark, sourly. 'I'm not quite right on these. It's as if I'm looking at myself from outside, detached, not really feeling anything at all . . .'

Rubbing both hands into his bloodshot eyes, he makes a waking motion as if he's been asleep for eternity. 'You shouldn't take them if they make you feel worse than before,' says the man. 'Adult life is better, although it probably doesn't feel like that right now, does it?'

'No,' you say, with a shrug.

'If I could change the past, I would. For years I've been chewing over every moronic choice I made at your age. That's why I'm sitting here now, with no proper place to live, unemployable, no family or friends, aside from the ones I made in there. And half of them'll end up back inside. But that doesn't stop me having a bit of hope. You have to have that, after all . . .' The man pauses, then clears his throat. 'If that doesn't sound too corny. I'm not a God-botherer or anything, as you've likely guessed . . .'

He flashes his knuckles, which are tattooed with devil's faces, and starts to grin; his teeth are nicotine stained and crossed at the front, with gaps along the side. You wonder if they were knocked out in a fight.

'You're a good one,' the biker says. 'But troubled. Then again, weren't we all troubled at eighteen?'

It will be another two hours before you reach the hospital, where your father is lying alone on a ward right now. Heat rises

CK ONE

as the motion of the coach and the odour of its chemical toilet add to the sense of dread.

For a few moments you manage to snatch sleep, your head resting on a scrunched-up jumper wedged against his shoulder, but you are awakened when he pulls his holdall from the storage.

'You shouldn't judge your parents as you'll probably make the same mistakes yourself one day,' he says. 'Mine are dead now. They should have been picking me up today.'

When he walks down the steps and onto the tarmac at the bus station, you feel a small pang of sadness in your belly.

'I hope your old man pulls through,' he mouths, waving goodbye from the foyer.

You watch him wander into the station, alone, where he pulls a packet of Rothmans from his jacket and lights up a smoke, inhaling deeply and exhaling with dragon rings.

LE MALE

Jean Paul Gaultier

Spotless white jeans. £100 belt. Crocodile loafers. Hair loosely permed. Anchor and chain inked on the bicep. Mermaids. Daggers. Swallow and roses. Screwing and drinking the main resolution. Salty scrubbed skin. Free-wheeling on shore leave. Butch exterior, treacle inside. Pleads for the day he can run back to sea …

It is the day of Steve Ward's funeral and there has been an early church service. Most of the pub's regulars have walked up to the cemetery, paying their last respects before the wake begins. Pat, the landlady, has prepared a spread in the back room of warmed-up sausage rolls, quiche Lorraine, and bowls of cheese & onion crinkle cuts. Unwrapping the packet of paper plates, you shuffle a pile of serviettes into a neat square, before returning to the bar, where a small queue has started to form.

Drying your hands with a towelling cloth, emblazoned with shire horses and the brewery's logo, you shake off the droplets, rubbing at the cracked skin on the edge of each palm. This morning, an envelope of £100 was left behind the bar to pay for the mourners' drinks, who are arriving shortly. In a town with three breweries, where the beer is subsidised, it works out at almost £1 a pint. Inside the social club, the price is even less. There is never a shortage of customers. Some work in the breweries, then spend most of their earnings in the pub. Before the brewery outlawed drinking on the job, most workers drank throughout the day as well.

Big Rodge, who your father worked with on the dray wagons, eats five cooked breakfasts every morning at the transport café before setting off on his round, nursing a pint at each delivery stop on the back roads of Yorkshire, Lancashire, Durham and beyond. Known as the Man Mountain, his capacity to sink vast quantities of ale still brings great delight to your father, who slows down his car to point whenever he passes Rodge in the street. You think he is secretly envious of his friend's ability to sink so much behind the wheel for decades without ever getting caught on the job. Like many around here, Rodge's belly resembles a beer barrel stuffed tightly beneath his shirt. Your father always says, 'all bought and paid for . . . he's still carrying twins', and often repeats his mantra with an extended smirk, 'strength goes in through the mouth'.

On weekends, the town's serious drinking begins on Friday night, and extends until the early hours of Monday morning, just before work begins. A routine that is rarely broken. It is not unusual to see drinkers staggering about at midday, with burning hot faces, lurching down the high street, already a quarter of the way through their regular cycle of fifteen pints a day. You know this because you serve them. When you mention this quantity to those from other places, they think you are exaggerating. Unlike some of the rumours you hear around town, this one is sadly true.

Some of your regulars are rake-thin, with exploded raspberry noses and have a peculiar, lurching walk, as if they are holding marbles in their underpants or shaking a used sock from the inside of their trouser legs. If they are lucky, they live until retirement. Most don't make it that far. And now their sons are of adult age, they too are following in their father's footsteps, although this time minus the jobs. Where once the breweries employed thousands of the town's residents, they now employ a few hundred. The retirees weren't replaced. Machines displaced workers. The only new contracts are short term. Just one independent brewery remains; the Popplewell Springs are finally running dry.

Edging around the bar, Pat polishes it with a cloth until it sparkles, her muscular arms almost pulling her polyester blouse away at the seams. Her heavily tinted hair is kirby-gripped aggressively to her scalp and keeps flopping into her eyes as she grimaces at the gunge spots flecked on drip trays evading her scrubbing brush.

LE MALE

'Bloody hell!' she sighs. 'Only midday and I'm already short of breath. Make sure you stock up the Britvic. How come you aren't up at the service anyway?'

'I didn't want to go up there again. Not after last time.'

'Not surprised. Well, it's only for other people. The dead don't care. He were a good customer, though,' she remarks, with a wistful tone. 'But funerals. I don't go unless I'm forced.'

Wiping down the lid of a pickled egg jar, you pause for a moment. It has been on the shelf so long the albumen has taken on a smoky blue tinge, yet the regulars prefer them this way. Vintage eggs soak up more alcohol, according to Barry, who eats one every day from a paper bun case along with a cling-filmed sliced ham and tomato bap for his lunch, with two pints of Ayingerbräu.

'Do you remember when Steve got in that state at New Year?' you reply to her. 'I heard him bawling his head off after last orders, and when I went outside there was nobody there. He was fighting thin air. Police found him snagged on the river bend. Jim reckons he'd thrown himself off the viaduct, that he'd been there for days already . . . His eyes had been eaten by the fish.'

'Fellas are lucky to make it to fifty around here,' Pat scoffs. 'You know what this place is like. Thankfully the women have more sense.'

You open a packet of beef and horseradish crisps, stuff them into two slices of white bread and margarine, then empty the dregs into your mouth. Folding up the packet into a small, tight triangle you aim it at the bin, letting out a long, prudent belch in tandem. Crumbs collect on your shoplifted Red or Dead mules which are starting to disintegrate from repeated beer splashes. Kicking them against the counter, you roll your sore ankle from side to side. It is still swollen from last week's accident: this time from falling down a full flight of stairs under the influence. The

BASE NOTES

swelling was the size of a large goose egg. It is still bandaged beneath your tights.

On the bar, four pints are lined up in a row, gently settling until the head is thick enough to top up. The staff are under strict instruction not to waste beer. Minor infractions are noted. You wait for a moment, then pull a few remaining drops of ambrosia into the tankards. Its maltiness is the smell that marks the pub, and the smell that marks the air outside. On brewing days hop clouds hang over the towers. It sticks to your clothes, hair and tastebuds. There is no escaping it.

As you rinse the ashtrays, a face appears through the window from outside. It is Darren.

He isn't like the other boys, Darren. There's always black sheep in every town, one that never fits in, no matter how hard they try. And you almost respect him for that. He is eccentric, obstinate and bizarre. Funny and annoying. One day he'll dress as a member of Wu-Tang Clan, the next in a pinstripe suit and bow tie. He is a man who intends to change the world, or at least leave the planet and fly to another.

Darren lives with his father, in a council flat tucked away on the far edges of town, within earshot of the dual carriageway. What you like about him, and perhaps what inspired your current brief romance, is the Jean Paul Gaultier fragrance he wears, Le Male. It is fashionable among the hard lads in town. Lavender . . . mint . . . artemisia . . . cinnamon . . . cardamom . . . orange . . . caraway . . . tonka bean . . . sandalwood . . . vanilla . . . amber and cedar . . . Even the hooligans wear it. That's how you first noticed him, over the bar. A scent that broke through the malty stickiness, his shaved head, Irish greeny grass eyes, and his laugh. At first, this was all attractive, but now even his cologne has started to grate.

LE MALE

As he unfastens his tie, mourners flock into the pub behind him and gravitate straight towards the bar. He quickly downs a pint, and mouths to you to call in on your way home. Light reflects from the copper-top tables, shimmering up onto the smoke-stained ceiling.

*

After closing the till, you walk down the high street, past the brewery, through a wet wind that seeps through your clothes. By the time you reach his place, your jacket is soaked. Darren has changed out of his funeral suit and is now wearing a dressing gown with a large red hood . . . and a bandana. He grins from the doorway, opens his dressing gown, and reveals a pair of Lycra cycling shorts, emblazoned with stars and stripes.

'You can't come in until you tell me who I am!' he cackles.

You shake your head and say, 'No clues?'

He starts rolling his head back, before jutting his pelvis forward and sticking his bottom out in a comic pose.

'You know where you are?!' he says, in a Yankee caterwaul.

'On your stairwell, Darren. Waiting to get in.'

'You're in the jungle, baby!' he yells. 'You're *gonna die*!!!!'

'Oh, very good . . . I'm sure Slash will be calling you before the year's out.'

He pulls his dressing gown back over his head, and leaps into the flat, doing his most painful Axl Rose impression, as if a cat is stuck in the door, howling to be released.

'So you're not too depressed about Steve, then?' you ask.

He flops down into his father's leather La-Z-Boy chair, with a rim of fading Brylcreem on the headrest, and pulls a sad clown face.

'Not really,' he groans. 'I mean, he were a laugh and that. But it's the second this month. It were worth going to for the free bar. Besides, it's what Steve would have wanted. A good send-off.'

Staring down at your feet, you pull at the saggy tights which have started to gather below your knees and drag them up until they tighten around your belly, a body part that is expanding by the week. Your own tolerance for beer has expanded along with its size. Customers often buy you a half on shift, which accumulates through the night. One for yourself, they often say. They feel more comfortable if you drink with them.

'Didn't you work with him on the canning line?'

'Yeah. He made it tolerable; it got so fucking boring standing there all day. We'd invent songs. Or imagine what we'd do when we won the lottery. I didn't realise he were that depressed.'

A malaise has washed through the town lately, with a wave of copycat suicides, drug addiction and petty crime. There is no such thing as counselling or therapy. Aside from being sent to Bootham Asylum, the black dog is not discussed.

You watch Darren as he presses the chair's armrest buttons and reclines backwards until the chair almost tips over. His milk bottle legs are above his head, and he rocks the chair, almost willing it to roll over on himself.

'How come you're dressed up as Axl, anyway?'

'To cheer meself up,' Darren says. 'And a surprise for you. Thought you liked GNR.'

'When I was thirteen, perhaps. But not now. These days I only listen to trip hop.'

Stifling a smile, you stare back into his face.

He replies, 'Too cool for heavy metal, are you? My, how you've changed. Don't worry. I won't tell anyone your dirty secret.'

You shuffle up from the sinking sofa and peer through the grubby nets onto the pavement below. The television is blasting by

LE MALE

the mantelpiece, Dale Winton's perma-tanned face is the brightest thing on *Supermarket Sweep*. A stacked pile of *X-Files* tapes is almost toppling on the carpet. Darren has spent the past week watching them all for the seventh time, convinced the episodes contain an important message that only he can crack. Next to the sofa is a large biscuit tin. It is rusting, but still has traces of the Cadbury logo on its lid.

'Mmmmm,' Darren says. 'I wonder what delicacies are inside?'

Crouching in a frog position, he sits next to you, balances on the cushions, opens the lid slowly and pushes it towards your face. You expect a collection of out-of-date garibaldis, pink wafers or soft rich teas. What is inside the tin is beyond your expectations.

'Euch! What the hell is that?'

The look of glee on Darren's face as he watches your revulsion is obvious.

'Beard shavings!' he sings, trying to contain his mirth. 'Frederico is a swarthy man, he needs two shaves a day . . . see, he has that shaver plugged in. Then, after he comes back from work, he shaves into the tin, then goes out drinking. The only thing is, he never empties the tin. There must be a year's worth in here.'

'Jesus. Thought my dad was bad. Are all divorced men like this?'

'It appears so.'

A queasy wave passes over you imagining the combination of skin and bacteria wafting beneath your face.

'Maybe their mothers loved them too much,' you say. 'Our fathers never learnt how to look after themselves.'

'Nah. It's just that life's too short to be tidying up. It's more fun down the pub, isn't it?'

In the kitchen, smeared grease lines the walls and windows. Fred's main cooking device, one sole blackened fat pan, is used every day to cook bacon, sausage, frozen beefburgers and on-the-turn tomatoes. It is never emptied. The antique lard that lines its base is around two inches thick. Each time you enter the room, your feet stick to the lino.

Rinsing a mouldy mug of tea out, you boil the kettle, and notice your side reflection in the mirror. Traces of dark foundation have collected around your ear. Like most of the women you know, you probably wear too much of it; but it's a useful mask, a way of disguising yourself from the real world, and a way of making yourself feel better if you're having a bad day, which for you, is most days at the moment.

'Don't you think it's a bit weird,' you shout to Darren, drying your hands on your skirt. 'You know, around here, recently. Death's meant to come in threes, but it feels like it's been coming in sixes.'

'A lot of them can't see what's beyond,' he replies from the fridge as he swigs flat Coke from a litre bottle behind you. 'The forces that control us. You see, for me, I'm going to be a famous actor. And a millionaire. Or a rock star. Or a rapper. Or the next Uri Geller . . .'

Becoming more animated with each mouthful, Darren belches his drink loudly, then says, 'But this lot, they don't want to go anywhere except here. They'll never travel to a higher plane. Apart from a night out at Basics. Then they come home on the first bus afterwards, and we all know what happens after that.'

You pause for a moment and think of the window seat where your friends used to sit nursing their comedowns on Sunday afternoons. Recently, they've stopped coming in. The pub is strangely subdued.

'Now Sammy's come back, she's started bringing gear in from Seacroft,' he says. 'That's really messed everything up. They aren't even bothering to go out. No more style, no more dancing.

LE MALE

Every Saturday's the same, a night in with the tin foil, a trip down brown town with Lou Reed. Dinner for one.'

The clock ticks erratically above the cooker, with the large hour hand sticking at 10. Its battery has needed replacing for months. Not that Darren or his father have noticed.

'Think I'm going to head back. Could do with an early night. I'm supposed to be starting work on the mural tomorrow.'

'Is that a smile I can see there?' says Darren.

'Yeah. It's the first thing I've looked forward to in ages.'

'It could do with not being used as a urinal.'

'That's what the landlord said as well. He's had a kids' slide delivered and they've laid a tonne of chipped bark. I popped over this morning. All the children'll be able to play in the beer garden so the parents can drink more in the pub. Only problem is, the slide's been pushed right against the wall. So when the kids use it, they splat straight into the brickwork.'

'A sly form of population control,' he laughs. 'I like it!'

'Haddy dropped off five tins of turquoise paint, so that's what I'm up to tomorrow. Painting the undercoat. Then, I've got these large pieces of cardboard from the brewery's delivery boxes. I asked the landlord's daughter to lie down on them, pulling jump and star positions, then I drew round her with a marker pen. After that, I cut them out. There's about seven of them in the pub's back garden. I'll use her as a template, with black paint around the shape and primary colours inside.'

Darren asks, 'What's the name of that artist you're copying?'

'Keith Haring. He made this mural called *Tuttomondo*, in Italy, just before he died from AIDS. We studied it in a lesson at college. What I'm making, it's a bit like it, but not exactly.'

'And you're getting paid . . . to paint this thing?'

'I know. Mad, isn't it. Actual money to paint a mural. The best thing is, it's going up in the most homophobic town in Yorkshire.

BASE NOTES

This is a truly wonderful thing, Darren. A proper statement. Nobody will have a fucking clue when they look at it. All those knuckle-draggers that drink in the pub. I've had to listen to their *opinions* for years. It's payback time.'

Pausing for a moment, you lean by the doorframe, with your handbag swinging from your shoulder, a gleeful expression washing over your face.

'You know what . . .'

'What?'

'This is going to be the most fun I've had for as long as I can remember.'

He leans over to kiss you on the ear, as you pull away, and zip up your coat.

'Come here,' he says. 'Can't you spare a few minutes?'

'No, I can't. Get off.'

'I've gone to all this effort. And now you don't want me. I've even sprayed meself with Le Male. Isn't that enough to give me a kiss?'

You turn your back on him, shake off his advances and reply, 'As much as I like you, Darren, I'm just not in the mood. I've other priorities. This mural, it's my passport out of this place. Besides, I've been at work and I stink.'

'It doesn't bother me,' he laughs, putting his hands around your waist. 'The riper the better.'

'We both know that's not true,' you say.

As you walk out the door, he calls behind you, 'If you don't want me now, well maybe we could go for a drink at the weekend instead? Pool at the Fox. Same time, same place?'

'Perhaps,' you reply, flippantly. 'If I feel like it. Which I probably won't.'

*

LE MALE

Later that night, you fill the bath with scalding water, steam clouds the room and clings to its blackened walls. Peeling your tights and knickers off, you throw them into the sink and quickly scrub them with a bar of Imperial Leather. Without a washing machine, all laundry is done by hand. In winter, you hang clothes to dry on the fireguard before bed. After your last falling-out, your mother has said you can't use her washing machine either.

In your father's house there are no carpets. You now live here with him two miles down a country road from the centre of town, in a hamlet without a phone box, bus stop or pavement to walk along. He wears a corset for his back due to the pronation in his missing foot and has rubber inserts for his shoes, so that he doesn't topple over from his lack of balance. Three years after his accident, he is still waiting for sick pay from the government which the authorities refuse to pay out. The lack of money means there is not enough to pay for a new fridge, sofa or clothes. Everything you own is scavenged or bought from the charity shop. A towel hangs over your draughty window, in place of a curtain.

When the back-boiler's water turns cold, you scatter a handful of Radox salts into the water. Plumes of sage and thyme rise from the water. Dropping your flagging body through the meniscus, you sink into the cloak of warmth below, pushing your face beneath the surface, embracing its stillness. One, two, three, you count, until finally reaching ten. Its blankness is a comfort.

As you rinse your hair, a crackling regional radio station slowly wafts up the stairs as the lamentable tones of Right Said Fred echo through the floorboards from the kitchen downstairs. Your teeth start to chatter as your rise from the water. You dry off with a still-damp towel that has the underlying tang of mildew and pull on a mauve fleece dressing gown. Rinsing stubble from the bath, you wrap the hairy plug around the taps, before clicking off the light switch. Outside, the moonlight beams brightly illuminating the crack in the curtains.

Climbing into your damp single bed as the pain in your ankle throbs, you start rubbing it beneath the sheets. The vision of tomorrow's mural is a beacon of light in an otherwise unendingly dour landscape. It is perhaps the only artistic statement you will ever be able to make here.

Not for the first time, your thoughts are starting to repeat, and you are exhausted by them. You are sick of yourself and sick of heading nowhere fast. This is not the adulthood you imagined, but there is no means of leaving, not yet. You are barely an adult but do not want to enter the same helpless hole that the rest of your friends have dug, because there is only one certainty living in a town like this: in Tadcaster, the only difference between a rut and a grave is the depth.

ANGEL

Thierry Mugler

Soda floats. Saint Tropez bronze. Platinum Ice Queen. Candyfloss lips. She walks the edge of a skyscraper roof, trying her luck at Manhattan Central Park. This thrill reminds her of fairground rides, the smalltown girl who wished upon a star. Bright lights, big city. Powder blue skies. Marshmallow, caramel, cookies & cream. Forever lost in a lucid dream...

You can always tell when Debs has entered the flat because the spice of her perfume arrives before she does. Her distinctive fragrance, the one that drips from each pore of her pale Penicuik skin, is Thierry Mugler's Angel. In the department store where she works, there is a large stand of the revolting stuff at the front of house. It is extremely popular in Edinburgh, the city where you now live. Vanilla and tonka . . . melon, pineapple . . . heliotrope . . . coconut . . . nutmeg . . . victoria plum . . . orange, blackcurrant . . . orchid and peach . . . caraway seed . . . patchouli in handfuls . . . hot chocolate . . . santal and amber . . . The sweaty walls of every nightclub drip with it.

Tonight, you are sitting on the sofa eating a small bowl of cornflakes from your lap, you have not eaten lunch or breakfast but have smoked fifteen cigarettes already. Billy, who you share the flat with, is taking Debs out to their usual drinking holes: Blue Moon Café for seven pints, then awful eurodisco at CC Blooms – the gay club at the top of Leith Walk.

She is wearing false eyelashes, a shimmering vest dress, butterfly clips in her hair, and a powder pink feather boa wrapped around her neck. But the most noticeable thing about her is the Angel. It is suffocating and fills every corner of the room like tear gas. Debs carries a bottle of it in her handbag, a purple glass star that she removes every hour and sprays liberally on her wrists and neck, as if it were an insect repellent in a hot country. Maybe it's a human repellent. It certainly repels you. There is something about the cloying fragrance that prompts waves of biliousness each time you encounter it. The bouquet has already infiltrated

BASE NOTES

your cereal, as you watch her flounce around the living room, dancing to Aqua's 'Barbie Girl', her anthem.

For the past few months, you have been staying here after Billy, a former colleague, took pity on your cause. He found you a job operating cashier tills in a shop on Princes Street and offered an air bed in his flat. 'You can't live out in the sticks, dear,' he said. 'You're far too fabulous for that.' Since December you've been sleeping in his walk-in wardrobe, tucked away in the corner of the room he shares with his boyfriend, Craig, an acerbic, withering English language student who is quietly furious at the new resident.

Together, you reside in a basement flat on Calton Hill. Luckily, it's a residence that will never suffer burglary due to the permanent armed police presence outside; the flat is discreetly hidden beneath the American Consulate. The rent is surprisingly cheap. How this has happened is a mystery to all who live here. There's John, the medical student, whose bedroom door is permanently closed, and Fang, the lesbian, who is getting thinner by the week. She is always arguing with her girlfriend and spends most of her time listening to Belle & Sebastian. Billy thinks she needs more Celine Dion in her life, and 'a good feed' at Valvona & Crolla. You like her. When she's not in, she lets you sleep in her bed, which is covered in fresh white cotton sheets. You have never slept under them before. Your unwashed mascara often stains her pillow, but she never complains.

As you finish the last spoonful from your bowl, Billy bursts through the door with two large bags of shopping. He has maxed out another credit card. This time, he has acquired a pair of snakeskin Patrick Cox loafers, black Levi 501s and a white linen shirt from Nicole Farhi to the sum of £364. He gives Debs two kisses on the cheek and says, 'You look gorgeous and ridiculous tonight. Give me ten minutes, and we'll be going.'

ANGEL

Sitting cross-legged on the armchair, Billy lights up a Marlboro Red, making an elegant Hollywood pose. You have never had a brother, but he's the closest to one that you'll ever have. He resembles Alain Delon, with long black eyelashes and aquamarine eyes. He is the most generous person you know but has a sting in his tail that is unleashed on unsuspecting victims. With him, you laugh the hardest.

Billy stares up at the curtains and raises an eyebrow. 'Them curtains need a good clean,' he laughs. 'That's a job for you at the weekend, young lady.'

'Well, I'm going out tonight, and I shan't be coming back until late,' you say.

'Oooh, hot date?' Debs squeals, as she twists the numerous rings on her fingers, holding them out towards the lamplight, enchanted by the sparkle.

'No. You see, I've been invited to tea up in Marchmont, by Juliette, one of Jo's friends, back in York. She lives in a student flat. I know her a bit. They're having a party, so that's where I'm heading.'

'Nae fun up there,' replies Debs. 'You shud come down CC's afterwards.'

Putting the bowl on the carpet, you pick up your guitar, one of the only possessions you own, strumming a few broken chords as you speak.

'Thought I should make myself scarce after last weekend.'

Billy starts to snigger, before launching into the camp mother character he often assumes when trying to tell you off. 'No, no, no. See, the thing is, *him* . . .'

He gestures to the room next door, where his boyfriend is reading quietly. Craig is annoyed that you still haven't found a place to live and have sponged off them for weeks. You can never afford the basics, toilet roll, washing powder or even food. But you can

BASE NOTES

always afford to go out drinking. It's a fair complaint. You are ashamed and don't know how to dig yourself out the hole. They are owed a big favour. Recently, they have started bickering at volume. It is probably your fault.

'Beautiful, charming Craig may look youthful, but he's a pensioner at heart,' declares Billy. 'So that message he left on the door was rather . . . *Hyacinth Bouquet* . . . I knew nothing about it . . .'

'I thought it was OK for me to stay, until I got on my feet,' you reply, uncertainly.

'It is!' Billy says. 'You're my friend. But you can't stay here for ever, otherwise he'll make my life hell. Can't you find a bedsit or something?'

Debs rolls her eyes and digs her elbow into Billy's side. She mutters, 'You cannae make her do that! Give her a break. She's only just landed.'

Billy looks you up and down, disapprovingly, then asks, 'Is that your outfit for tonight?'

'I don't have much else to wear, just these tights, tatty jumper, old jacket . . .'

For a moment, you pull on the leather necklace with a silver nine-pointed star around your neck. It has an all-seeing eye in the middle which you believe radiates magic powers, or at least makes others believe you are psychic. Recently, you've acquired a set of Tarot cards, which are resting on the bookcase. For the past few days, you have been learning the three-card spread. You keep drawing the Tower, Ten of Swords and Five of Cups when you read for yourself, which apparently you shouldn't do, along with smoking or drinking around the cards. You are convinced something awful is about to happen and the cards know something you don't.

Debs downs a vodka and cranberry in one go before declaring

ANGEL

she is ready to head into the night. The boisterous pair vanish through the front door, singing in tandem until there is silence. You pull out a mirror, reapply a splodge of liquid eyeliner, pick up your keys, and stare at the note in your pocket with a telephone number scribbled on it.

*

An hour later, you walk out of the flat and head down towards Waverley, passing the wet blackened sandstone of the old Royal High School, a vast building with Doric columns overlooking Arthur's Seat, the extinct volcano just down the road. Every morning, bagpipes start playing at Holyrood at daybreak, the soundtrack to the Queen's mostly empty residence. It is torturous with a hangover. As much as you like living in this strange new city, you cannot, and will not, ever tolerate the sound of a deflating bagpipe. You have convinced yourself it is what hell sounds like. Tonight, around twenty pipers are having another session. The sound makes your ears melt.

Walking quickly along the A1 towards Princes Street, you escape the cacophony. Even with gloves, your hands are freezing cold, and your breath makes rich plumes in the crisp evening air. Although the speed of your steps is warming, you have wrapped a scarf around your head up towards your nose, and regret wearing a short skirt this evening. Your legs are cold, even wearing 60 denier tights. What is really required is a hat and long coat. Auld Reekie in winter is the coldest place you have ever been, the wind so brutal it climbs up the inside of your thighs, chilling you to the bone. When you have enough money, you'll buy proper clothes. Nobody warned you about the temperature up here.

BASE NOTES

Arriving at the tenement, you observe the kitchen is full, although the living room is cold and empty. Juliette gives you a hug as you drop a carrier bag of four cans of Foster's onto the bench.

With her long hair swishing in the draught of an open window, she asks, 'Would you like a drink?' Hers is the sort of hair that gets caught in shop doors. She has cheeks like pink apples and powder blue eyes. Her dress is a faded cotton bridal gown from the Victorian era which she wears with a pair of 28-hole boots.

'I've brought beer,' you reply.

'Have some wine instead,' she insists, then pulls you into the kitchen, introducing you to her friends. They are students, like her, and have voluminous, gentrified southern accents. These are people who do not talk like you, in fact, it's almost like they are speaking a different language altogether. Right now, they are having an intense discussion about something called Cartesian duality.

Juliette says, 'This is Tom, he's studying philosophy with Wilf. And this is Bea, who I share the flat with, she's an "art dosser" like me. And this, this is Seb, who's studying classics.'

They all say hello, and you say hello back.

'And what are you reading?' Seb asks.

You fall quiet for a second. Asking what someone is reading is a bit peculiar after you've just been introduced. Attempting to think of books you might have read that will make you sound intelligent, you blurt out, *'Zen and the Art of Motorcycle Maintenance*!'

Everyone in the kitchen starts to laugh, and you don't understand why.

'That's not what I meant,' he replies, shaking his head, before pouring a large glug of wine into his glass, filling it to the brim. 'You know, reading, as in . . . studying. What subject are you studying?'

ANGEL

Shuffling about on the stool, you stare out of the window and try to think of the right thing to say.

'I'm not, I just work in town. But I did go to college, that's where I met Juliette, on foundation. I have a GNVQ level 3 in media studies.'

Seb's eyes squint as he pushes his glasses up the bridge of his long, thin nose. 'I suppose there's a subject for everyone,' he laughs. 'Is there much call for that working in Topshop?'

Within minutes of arriving, you have been determined as a person of little value or use, and when they all start speaking French to each other, you feel even more out of place. If you listen carefully, you can decipher the occasional word, but you are certain they are doing it as a way of not talking to you. Seb keeps gesturing as if he is Italian and saying what must be very witty phrases as all the others are laughing along with him.

They are now serving spaghetti from a giant pan, which Juliette has poured a jar of tomato sauce into. She serves seven bowls of it, sprinkling Parmesan onto the top, then pours oil on each bowl. You've never eaten oily pasta before, only Pasta 'n' Sauce from a packet. This is the first dinner party you have been to, and tonight you decide it will be your last. Only middle-class people on TV sitcoms have dinner parties; it is not something that happens at home. You are starting to regret coming here and wonder how long you will last before you can make an excuse to leave. Right now, you are lost without any map home.

*

By 8.30 you have already spent an hour in Juliette's kitchen, before deciding on a shrewd move, shrinking back into the night before anyone notices you are gone. You pick up your jacket, surreptitiously pushing a packet of Seb's fags into the pocket, and slip down towards the corridor.

'Had enough of us already, have you?' Juliette sings with her purple wine smile, swaying in the kitchen doorway as you attempt to open the sticky lock. 'You need to push it to the left.'

'Sorry,' you say. 'I'm supposed to be meeting my friend in town.'

'Maybe we can go for a drink sometime? Have a catch-up?'

'Thanks for inviting me. I'll make sure to call you.'

The sense of relief when you walk down the stairwell is overwhelming. It feels as though you've been diving underwater without an air tank for the past hour. Once outside, you start to breathe properly again, and head towards the phone box, pulling out the piece of paper in your pocket. It has Ali's number on it. He works in the suit sales department at work and now you share tea and smoke breaks together in the kitchen upstairs.

When you call him from the phone box, to your great relief he picks up straight away. Ali says he'll come and meet you in the City Café on Blair Street, a place he knows well. You are glad he said yes. He's one of the only people you can talk to properly since arriving in this cold, unforgiving city of shadows.

*

The Royal Mile is busy when you arrive. A few rowdy drunks stagger about. Heading up the steep road towards City Café, you can see Ali is waiting in the window, supping a pint of lager. He waves at you, then gestures towards the bar. When you enter, he has already lined one up for you. It is a fifties-style diner serving soda floats during the day and red leather booths facing out onto the street.

ANGEL

'Thank fuck you picked up the phone. What a nightmare that was . . .'

He pulls on his tennis shirt collar and leans back into the seat.

'What happened?' he asks.

'Nothing, really. But everything as well. It's been a funny week. I'm all out of sorts.'

'Are you all right?'

You slurp on the fizzy lager as its bubbles burst up the inside of your nostrils.

'I think so. It's just . . . I was invited up to Marchmont . . . then it all went a bit wrong . . .'

Ali starts to laugh, then shakes his head, and grins. 'You dinnae want to go up there,' he says. 'Too many students. You shud stay in the safe place, which is Leith, of course.'

He puffs his chest out, waiting for you to agree.

'Up there, they made me feel like I was thick. And I don't normally feel like that. And they all talked posh. And in French! I mean, who does that?'

Ali leans forward and rests his head on his open palms, his dark curly hair shining in the light, and listens carefully to everything you say.

'Pay them no mind,' he says. 'They're all higher up the ladder. They don't talk like us because they're no like us at all. Another species altogether. You shouldnae worry. Who cares about them?'

'It's just . . . I'd never thought about it, you know, not fitting in.'

'Truth be told, it's not about fitting in with them,' he says. 'You're from another culture.'

As you listen to what he is saying you wonder about the difference between you and them, a polarity you've never considered before. Ali is older than you and appears to understand the ways of the world. Especially around here. Last summer, he travelled to North Africa and stayed with the Bedouin where he lived on blood and milk out in the desert. He has a handmade tattoo on his forearm that you have never noticed as he always wears a shirt and tie at work. It says CCS.

Running your fingers across the letters, you ask: 'What does that stand for?'

He winces a little, then says, 'You really wannae know?'

'Cold cabbage soup?'

After a few seconds, he starts talking quietly. 'I used to run with Hibs when I was younger. Y'ken? A firm. Probably a bit like some of your pals at home.'

'What, like the Service Crew?'

'Aye, a bit like that, I suppose. I dinnae bother with them nae more. It got too much in the end. I'm no really a violent type. And besides, the rave scene came in and a load of us started doing that instead.'

You squeeze his hand and smile at him, before kicking his feet gently under the table. Then you say, 'Sounds about normal. It changed everything back home as well, gave them all summat to do. At least they stopped booting each other's heads in for a sport.'

'We had a few scrapes back in the day. Now I'm just a scarfer. It's easier that way.'

'You could take me on a hot date to Easter Road if you want . . . in the rain . . .'

Ali shuffles to one side and digs into his jeans pocket, pulls out his wallet and opens it on the table.

'That'd be braw. Does this mean we're on a date?'

'Maybe it does,' you say, as your cheeks turn red.

'Do you want half a pill? The night is young.'

For a moment you consider returning to the flat or spending the rest of the night being tortured by Man 2 Man with Billy and

ANGEL

Debs on a sticky discotheque dancefloor. The decision is made. You stick out your tongue, then close your eyes as he splits a sour tablet in two, dropping it into your mouth.

Swilling down his sacrament with two gulps of lager, you say, 'The Body of Christ.'

'Amen, Sister,' he replies.

*

You arrive back at Billy's flat just after dawn. Ali walks you up Leith Walk after an encounter with one of his friends who invited you back to his place after the lock-in closed. The tenement had bare floors, one broken sofa and a congealed toilet without a seat. Ali's friend was called Mikey and kept babbling onto himself about 'booting the fuck out of the huns'. In the coldest moments before dawn, he was intimidating, and only after he smoked a blackened foil of brown, and rolled off to sleep on his sheetless mattress, did you and Ali get some time alone together.

You had been drinking all night, and had just enough drugs to make everything sparkle, but not enough to make you gurn or retch. Neither of you were trying to be erotic, there were no theatrics, but lying together barely clothed on Mikey's sticky stained sofa, wrapped in each other's arms, it felt like some kind of intimacy. In a moment of deeper sleep, Mikey woke the pair of you up in his half-perished underpants, saying you were 'a hoor' and Ali was 'a fucking cunt' and you needed to leave before he brained the pair of you. All you remember are his crumbling buck teeth barking in your face, and the hot stink of his breath still humming from the cascade of roll-ups he'd chain-smoked before bed, that and the soiled residue of his unwashed armpits. Half-asleep, half terrified, you quickly pulled your clothes on, as Mikey's face twisted into that of a poisonous reptile in the seconds before an attack.

When the sun came up, the biting easterly wind chased you from behind, whipping through the streets as you rattled up the road from Mikey's flat, both of you stinking from last night's drinking. Ali made sure you did not walk back alone.

Now, you are standing outside Billy's flat, and the city is yawning into Sunday morning life. The slightest hint of traffic rumbles on the road below the park. A bright orange sun starts to rise from the east, casting its light on your faces.

'Is this the moment when I'm allowed to starting singing "Sunshine on Leith"?'

'There's never a right time to sing The Proclaimers,' you say, 'unless you've had a skinful. And your skinful has worn off, so there's no excuse.'

'I'm sorry about my pal. He shouldn't have said that. Mikey's a total dick sometimes.'

You stare into his eyes, which are reddened from the all-night session, with dark rings beneath, and start touching his face. Resting your head on his chest, you listen to his heartbeat for a moment, then whisper, 'I figured he was one of your old mates. It's hard to shake them off sometimes.'

He wraps his arms around you, strokes your hair, which has started turning greasy.

'I'll nae come in. Your flatmates will be asleep. I know it's not easy living down there . . .'

It occurs to you right now in this moment, even if it is an intoxicated one, that Ali wants nothing from you other than your company, and treats you with respect, even though you are younger than him. You know it is going to hurt saying goodbye, because if you were going to stay in this city, it would be here,

ANGEL

with him. You do not tell him this is the only night out together you will ever have.

As you pull the keys from your bag, he waves, then leans forward, and kisses you gently on the cheek. He walks off into the distance whistling to the wind. You wave, then step back into the flat that still reeks of Angel perfume and wonder if you should have followed him after all.

EARTHWORM

Demeter

Barefoot children running through paddocks. Hands in the loam. A bull's liver plough. Writhing earthworms slide on the spade. Dew on the grass. Old English oak. A comforting fog of warm petrichor. Orchard branches. Compost and mulch. Ragwort verges. Old twine rope. Hair tangled in celandine stems...

After dressing the department store window one dreich Tuesday morning, you decide it is finally time to visit New York. Head office's styling theme for the week is the Exploding Plastic Inevitable and you have spent the previous hour hanging tinfoil panels from the ceiling and setting the timer for an oil lamp which projects swirling psychedelic visuals at nightfall, illuminating the dank pavements of Briggate. Draping a sequinned fish-scale dress from the mannequin's sharp shoulders, you start taping an Afro wig onto her lacquered bald head and glue a pair of drag queen lashes onto her polished eyelids.

'Manhattan. Maybe I'll find my destiny there,' you say to your co-worker, Leo, hooking an arm into place. 'Warhol was a window dresser, that's how he started. There's flights going for ninety-nine pounds. Maybe I should go and stay at the Chelsea Hotel for my birthday? I can be a superstar for the week.'

He looks across with a bemused expression and starts grinning. 'New York's not what you think it is, love. It's changed since the disco days. Although apparently Andy started out on the shit-heap as well, so there's hope for us yet . . .'

'Talk about killing the dream,' you reply.

Outside on the street a small gang of teenage girls in puffer jackets are staring through the window, blowing condensation onto it, and squashing their faces up against the glass. You smile sweetly back at them, give them the finger, then crawl up through a small doorway before setting the projector lights from the shop floor. Leo places the sale vinyl onto the glass, tears off its backing and squeegees lettering onto the pane.

BASE NOTES

'I'm not saying don't go,' he spits. 'You just might need to plan, that's all. It's not like Leeds, you know.'

Brushing dust from your trousers, you shout down to him, 'Well, I'm going!' in a voice so loud that two customers tut on the shop floor behind you, before making a complaint to the manager. It is the second time you have been reported this week.

*

Still tingling from the previous night's excess, you clip the seat belt into place on the aircraft. The best course of action is one of Dutch courage, so you promptly take advantage of free vodka on Virgin Airways. It is the first time you have ever flown alone, but their pre-Millennium coupon deal was an opportunity too good to miss. Wearing a stretch tight Buddha print top and flared trousers with a broken zip held in place with a safety pin, your dishevelled appearance contrasts against those of your fellow travellers, who are quiet, besuited businesspeople. One pulls a sleeping mask over his face to avoid your incessant talking.

Your clothes carry a trace of Demeter's Earthworm, a fragrance you have a sample of from the perfume counter at work. In exchange for polishing signage, building displays and designing the most eye-catching stands, you have been given a handful of glass vials from this new brand, one which repulses the wealthy cream and gold clientele of North Leeds who shop there. They often have grimaces and shocked faces as they squirt the novelty fragrance onto testing strips. 'Disgusting!' one said. 'Despicable!' said another. 'What kind of person would wear anything as vile as this?'

Already, you have worked your way through Demeter's unusual range: Tomato, Crayon and Tarmac. Smelling like real life

EARTHWORM

is a contrast to all the heavy, migraine-inducing scents of your mother's salon in the 1980s. Your favourite is Earthworm . . . cut grass . . . petrichor . . . soil tincture . . . rotting leaves . . . It is redolent of dewy mornings, or the paddocks surrounding your father's home and the soft allure of spring. Wearing Earthworm makes you not forget where you came from, no matter how much you are part of the city right now.

After sunrise, you begin the descent into Newark, and a wave of tiredness washes through your body. Unbeknown to you, the chaos is only beginning. Freewheeling in New York is the sort of mistake you only make once before swearing to never ever be unprepared again.

Following a humiliating run-in with passport control, and numerous failed attempts to board a bus, you arrive at Port Authority in a state of shell shock. The city's streets flash by; each block tall and ominous, blocking out daylight and compressing pedestrians. As a person with no real comprehension of numbers, jet lag adds to your lack of bearings. The absence of street names or noticeable landmarks is disorienting. Billboard posters of WWF, Lauryn Hill and *American Beauty* line the main avenues. Never mind, you tell yourself. You'll check into the room and sleep it off.

When you arrive at the Chelsea in the pouring rain, you are informed at reception that your room has been double-booked. This is apparently your fault for not confirming the booking, as requested. Not that you recalled them telling you that. Sitting in the lobby's faded seats, you plead with the staff, but they inform you it's Fashion Week and all the vacant rooms were booked by Vivienne Westwood months ago. They have no record of your name or any deposit paid.

For a few minutes you sniffle in the foyer, on the precipice of

BASE NOTES

throwing an almighty tantrum, then storm out of the hotel and start walking the streets. Raindrops bounce off concrete, flooding the drains beneath. A deep rotten stench rises upwards from each subway vent that you pass.

Hurricane Floyd is heading towards the city; the rains are the first indication of the wild storm that will hit in the next few days. You should have checked the weather before departing. Or perhaps confirmed where you were going to stay. There are many things you should be doing right now; a litany of small catastrophes could easily be avoided, were you not infected by the recklessness of youth. This year, you have been convinced that you won't make it past twenty-five years of age. Mistakes don't matter if you aren't going to live long enough to face their consequences.

*

Two long hours later, after drinking bottomless coffee in a diner, then traipsing around Madison Square Park in sodden clothes, you stop outside a hotel that looks almost dishevelled enough to be affordable. Even this modest accommodation is $180 for a walk-up rate, an impossible price for a bed. You sit on the pavement outside the hotel, watching wealthy ladies walk Pomeranians on long, elegant leather leads. Feeling like Joe Buck in *Midnight Cowboy*, you are a hillbilly lost in the city, with no Ratso in sight. At least Joe Buck had a room, even if it was fleeting. You tell yourself any flea-infested pit would be better than the saturated streets you will most likely sleep on tonight.

Peeling the film from a pack of cigarettes, you ask the porter if you can shelter beneath the foyer. He grins and nods his head.

'You've been hanging out here for too long,' he says. 'Don't get yourself into trouble.'

EARTHWORM

The porter's name is Tito. He has an attractive gap between his front teeth and glinting grey eyes. He takes pity on you. After a few minutes of talking to him in fake RP honed from childhood elocution lessons, rather than your native tongue, he warms up.

'See, you can't stay out here all night. Not a real lady like yourself. But there's a hostel on the Upper West Side. Let me ask reception if we can call them for you.'

He vanishes into the hotel and emerges ten minutes later with a scrap of paper.

'You're in luck, Miss English Girl. Here's the address, but the thing is, they don't have no space tonight. They have a bed from tomorrow afternoon. If you bunk it won't cost too much.'

'I can't thank you enough,' you say. 'This is perfect. But it's getting late. Is there a place I can go in the meantime? Like a café or something?'

Waves of sickness wash over you. Fuzzy streetlights glitter in your peripheral vision and slowly sway like a kaleidoscope. Sleep is urgently required. Your brain is capsizing.

Tito replies, 'Most cafés shut around here after midnight. But listen, if you're really stuck, I clock off at two a.m. We could grab a coffee if you don't mind walking half an hour or so. I know an all-night place. But . . . you could always stay with me. I live with my sister. You can have my bed. I'll take the couch . . .'

For a split-second you doubt your ability to make the right decision but have little choice when faced with a night at a stranger's house or a night on the streets sleeping under pizza boxes.

'Sure,' you say, before making a nervous smile. 'That would be wonderful . . . if you don't mind me lodging for a few hours? Promise I'll behave.'

He grunts and pulls up his collar and tie, before saying a few words under his breath, almost like a prayer: 'You can be my guest.'

BASE NOTES

In the small hours, Tito clocks off from work and takes you on a rattling train to South Bronx, then onto Longwood Avenue. You walk out of the subway steps and into the street. It is still dark, but the world is waking up.

'You know, lady, you might wanna take that coat off.'

'Why?' you reply, pushing a pellet of chewing gum into your mouth that has started to taste like a three-day-old sock.

'Because this is my hood, and well, I'm not being nasty or nuthin', but you might get stared at, and I don't want you runnin' into any trouble down here.'

Stopping outside a laundromat, you check out your leather coat in the window's reflection, which you believe, despite the torn Afghan collar, to be quite stylish.

'It's my only coat and I'm freezing,' you whine. 'What's wrong with it?'

Tito starts to peel off his jacket and hands it to you.

'Just take the coat off, OK, you can borrow mine until we reach my place. If you wear that around here, you'll draw attention to us. And we don't want anyone looking, trust me.'

'Ooh, this place is like in the movies. *The Warriors.* Or *Wild Style.*'

Tito's face lights up.

'Man, you seen *Wild Style*?'

'Uh-huh. Do you think we could buy some grass?'

'Mmmm. Later. The shop ain't open now, if you catch my drift.'

As you walk over the crossroads and along the low-rise tenement blocks, you complain that your feet are hurting.

'You'll need to get new kicks tomorrow,' he says. 'Otherwise they'll know you ain't from here.'

There is an unusual power to him, now you are walking in his neighbourhood. Faces nod to him, and he nods back. Street kids scatter as he heads towards them.

EARTHWORM

'Are there gangs around here?'

He starts to laugh, shaking his head.

'You could say that, yeah.'

'What, like guns and drugs and crime?'

'That's the reputation. Over there in England, you have no idea.'

'Leeds is rough, you know!! I live in Burley. The most burgled postcode in Europe . . .'

'That ain't no comparison to the Bronx. You wanna know why I'm a porter?'

'I just presumed you liked the job.'

'No. I don't *like the job*, but I have to do it, because it's part of my parole. See, I've been inside for years. Six weeks ago, I was in Rikers . . . just over the water . . .'

He rattles a pair of keys in his pocket and walks towards a doorway.

'You heard of the Latin Kings? Well, I ran with that crew. And I got into trouble, young. If you ain't educated then it's hard to escape this place.'

As you ascend the stairs into a block, his hand brushes against your back.

'Listen, before we go in, my sister's not gonna be pleased you're here. Just keep your head down and I'll deal with her. She's got work to go to. Stay in my room until I say so.'

Opening the door which has been kicked in numerous times and repaired with splodges of plaster, he quietly guides you along the corridor. You glimpse the walls patterned with torn-off paper, and the cavities behind it. Then the noise begins.

'Who the fuck is that?!' his sister shouts. 'You brought that piece of cracker shit back with you?'

Then the pair descend into an incendiary argument, the likes of which can only ever take place between siblings.

BASE NOTES

Hiding from the racket, you perch on the edge of his single canvas bed and stare down at the pavements below, watching children playing beneath a broken water hydrant as sunlight breaks through the clouds. His bedroom is decorated sparsely, with one large poster of Tupac Shakur above the pillow and a neat collection of used flycatchers hanging from the window frame, coated with cadavers of dried bluebottles.

The front door slams, then he comes into the bedroom with a glass of water.

'She's gone now. I brought you a drink.'

'Thanks,' you reply, wondering how to escape from the apartment now that his sister has gone. 'Can I look around?'

'Yeah, the main room is in here . . .'

He gestures towards the corridor, then the living room, where a floral sofa has plastic covers zipped over the suite. In one corner, a hospital bed is perfectly made, with a drip by its side. A model of the Virgin Mary is placed on a shelf above the bedhead, with candles and rosary beads hanging from her open hands.

'Can I crash in here, then?'

'You ain't sleeping in here,' he replies, with a level of irritability. 'This is my mother's bed.'

'Oh. Is she out?'

'She's dead,' Tito says, removing his shoes.

'Sorry.'

'Thanks, but you didn't know her. My sister nursed her in here. She died in this room. We keep it to remember her by.'

You listen to the clock tick, staring up at the photographs taped to the wall.

'You can have my mattress. Let me know if you get cold.'

There is an awkward pause as you turn towards the doorway. He stands a little too close for comfort, staring as you bend down to pick up your bag.

EARTHWORM

'You want a shower?' he asks.

'Erm . . . that would be great . . .'

'There's a towel through there.'

As you walk into the bathroom, you let out a sigh, only to notice the lack of a physical door. An almost see-through curtain covers the shower. You check the corridor, disrobe, put your clothes in a pile, then step into the hot stream, pushing your face beneath it, soaping your sweating body down. The water is blissful, until you turn to rinse, and see him watching you through the door, licking his lips.

'Sure you don't want some help in there?' he asks.

You shake your head and pull the curtain as far as it can reach as he slinks back into the dark.

The watching continues as you sleep in his bed, his presence hovering above as you pull the sheets tightly over your shoulders. Your heart thumps into your throat each time he appears, but you force yourself to act as if you are in the deepest slumber. At one point you can hear him breathing slowly onto your neck, his shadow moving across your face.

You have no idea where you are, no mobile phone or means of calling for help. His sister is out; he could rape you, rob you, take your passport, and nobody would know what had happened. Your friends warned you not to travel alone, and this is the reason why. It is the first time you have ever been aware of your own mortality. Playing Sleeping Beauty is your only form of protection. If he knows you are awake, you could die.

Despite your frigid body, deep inside, your brain chatters to itself. It repeats, 'This is all your own fault. You flirted with him so that he took pity on you. Then you laughed at his jokes, squeezing his arm on the train. You revealed too much about yourself. Took too much interest in what he had to say. There is no wonder he thinks he's in luck. You shouldn't be surprised that he's trying it on. If you'd been level-headed this would never have happened in the first place.

    Your fault.
    Your fault.
    Your fault.

Sleeping is uncomfortable with money rolled up inside your bra pads, and REM lasts for five minutes at a time, before adrenaline wakes you with its shock. You lie still, until you hear him boiling water hours later; only then do you leave the safety of his bedsheets, which you have tightly cocooned around your body like a chrysalis.

    'Can I take you out for breakfast?' you ask, as he washes the morning dishes. 'To show my appreciation?'

    'If you want. That's kind of you. It should be me taking you out, though . . .'

    He hangs his head and shrugs his shoulders.

    'I'm ashamed I can't pay,' he says.

    'Don't worry about that, I mean, your place is cheaper than a hotel room. I can't thank you enough.'

    'I tried to sell some diesel first thing, on the corner. Before you woke up. So I could take you out. But there was nuthin' goin' on out there. I'm afraid my pockets are empty.'

    'Oh,' you reply. 'Didn't realise you were dealing.'

    'It's hardly a great career move, huh? But needs must.'

Before his night shift begins, Tito returns you to Central Park, dropping you off at the hostel. He spent the previous hour saying how he doesn't want to let you go. In his view, you are made for each other, the stars are aligned. In your view, you want to flee as quickly as you can. So of course, to wriggle out of the situation,

EARTHWORM

you arrange to meet him the following day to watch the boxing at his flat. A date that you have zero chance of following through on.

Carrying your case up the hostel steps, he puts his hand on yours, holding it gently.

'Do I get a kiss?'

You lean forward and peck him on the cheek.

'There you go!'

'A proper one?'

There is an awkward pause before you cough and look at an imaginary watch.

'Sorry, have to go! Time to check in.'

He turns slowly, raising his fist to the air as he starts walking down the staircase.

'See you tomorrow, then,' you shout after him.

'I ain't seeing you again, dime piece,' he grumbles, walking off into the trail of traffic.

*

Days become nights for the next few days, and you are only woken by your Antipodean roommates' clattering as they come and go on their daily expeditions. By night, you eat noodles from paper boxes on the roof terrace, just like in the movies. By day, you wander aimlessly around Greenwich Village, in the hope that someone will talk to you, or at least give you some directions.

You have no idea who you are, where you are going, or what day of the week it happens to be, and that's back home, never mind here, in an alien land. Recently, weekends have been all-encompassing and consuming, to such an extent that you are barely capable of holding down a job. It is likely there will be no job left at all when you return to England, judging by your accumulation of written warnings.

BASE NOTES

Even without jet lag, since turning twenty-two, your brain has turned to wet flour. Each Monday morning feels like climbing from the wreckage of a car crash, but even that isn't enough to stop you returning to the vehicle and driving it off the bridge again and again and again. Your waist is almost small enough to fit into two large hands, your arms like those of a porcelain doll, and here in New York, you can fit into tiny jeans from the 1970s. The thinner you become, the more powerful you feel.

Back home in Leeds, you share a house with a convent schoolgirl, a friend with a far more substantial tolerance for intoxication than yourself. Keeping up with her professional intake is not for the faint of heart. And although you live in a damp and dingy back-to-back, your dank red-brick terrace is decorated with tropical flowers which you procure from the department store's dustbin each week, bringing light to the gloomiest corners.

Inadvertently, you have joined a party of revellers who are educated, with social polish. Most come from professional families and stable homes. Your new friends can even afford to buy cocaine. They have dinner parties, play board games and know about wine. Their shelves are lined with classic literature. They have travelled to places like Tibet, Koh Samui and Rio de Janeiro. You are envious of their stories, and in return you have tried to keep up. Predictably your mind and body have started to unravel.

You reflect on the mess as you traipse the Lower East Side streets, swearing to change for the better, should you make it out alive. At any given time, you can barely comprehend which direction you are heading. Your only saving grace comes from record shops, where at least you feel at home, and can talk about music to the staff. The universal language of vinyl is useful, an East Village reggae shop becomes your compass, and from there, with the assistance of customers who take pity on you, pathways are drawn

EARTHWORM

on envelopes, maps are pushed into your hand, and you begin to navigate your way around the city.

Being in New York for the first time, alone, is a sensory overload. Every TV series you watched obsessively as a child, every film, every record, every piece of art – they all connected and fed back to these streets, as if you were destined to be here all along. You have always imagined travelling across the Atlantic, but the experience of arriving here is deflating. The illusion superior to reality. Some New Yorkers are the rudest people you have ever met, yet others help in a way that is beyond what you deserve. This is an extreme environment, with no place to relax, or to hide from the crowds. For two concurring days, you spontaneously weep, before calling home out of desperation.

'I'll send you some money,' your mother says, down the end of the line as you sob into the receiver of a urine-soaked phone booth. 'Let me book you a flight back . . .'

'No, Mum, I need to ride this out. It's something I have to do on my own.'

'But I can hear how stressed you are. I'll raid the shop takings and send you enough to bring you home. Honestly, I don't know why you bothered! You could have just gone to Greece like everyone else.'

'I don't want to go to Greece!' you wail.

'You're such a snob! A cheap beach and sunshine break would've done you the world of good. Holidays aren't supposed to be stressful . . .'

As much as you protest, you have to concede she is right.

'I know that now, and I know you're looking out for me. But I'm going to stay for a few more days . . . I saw the Lennon memorial in Central Park last night. It's not all bad.'

'What about that hurricane? We saw it on the news. Have you any waterproofs?'

BASE NOTES

'Yes, of course,' you lie. 'It's started up now. Shop awnings turning inside out, even the drains are spewing. Look, Mum, I've got to go. At least you know where I'm staying. If I get murdered, you can send the police to find me.'

She starts to chuckle and clears her lungs with a big phlegmy cough.

'Huh-huh-huh-huhhhhhh.'

'I'll be back home next week. Promise.'

You hang up, then walk out into the tumultuous storm that is raging in Chinatown. Waves of water rinse down the tarmac, as yellow taxis spray puddles onto irate pedestrians. Fleeing the deluge, you hide inside a DIY shop and feel rainwater pooling in your trainers as you attempt to dry off in the doorway. A tall man is bent over, looking at rolls of reflective vinyl.

Leaning down to shake off your coat in the doorway, you say, 'Unusual pattern. A bit like my gran's pantry floor.'

He turns and beams up at you, before pulling a length out into the light.

'You could say that. It looks like you've been caught?'

'Are you from London?'

'Well spotted,' the man says, removing his spectacles, wiping condensation from them.

His pale linen shirt is damp and sticks to his body. He has grey hair, and silver jewellery, but nothing too ostentatious. These are designer clothes. He looks and smells expensive, as if he is wearing ambergris on his wrists today.

You ask, 'How come you're in here?'

'That's a good question, I should ask the same of you . . .'

'Oh. Well, it's a bit random.'

He looks your outfit up and down slowly, as if he is assessing your attire.

'That's a curious ring. Is it ceramic?'

EARTHWORM

Holding your hand up towards him, he runs his finger around the rim. It has a painted scene of the crucifixion, with Mary Magdalene praying at his feet.

'I think so, yes. I'm going through a Catholic phase right now, it's very chic!'

The man laughs and shakes the dampness from his shirt, wafting it against the air conditioning unit that rattles and groans overhead.

'Not chic if you were raised in it, believe me. Really, though, what brings you to New York?'

'Andy Warhol. It was his idea. You see . . . I work in department stores, building interiors, that sort of thing. And I don't get paid much. And it's a bit boring at times. When I'm working, I like to pretend that I'm someone else, or living in another time. Because my real life's a bit shit. And I've no money. There's not much alternative so you just put up with your lot. Then I remember that being a window dresser is the most creative job I'll ever have because I don't have qualifications or know anyone important, so I should appreciate what I've got. Above my bed I've this postcard of Andy Warhol, and books about him on my shelf. I think about him a lot. And the Factory. So that's why I'm here. Even though he's dead . . .'

'*Searching for Warhol*,' he replies. 'The title of your memoir one day . . .'

'What's your name, then?'

'Oh, how rude. I'm Tom.'

'Hi, Tom. You have fabulous shoes . . . How come you're here anyway? Sorry to ramble on . . . I get a bit carried away with myself . . .'

Tom strokes his chin and makes a quiet humming sound before answering.

'I am here for Fashion Week,' he groans. 'And I hate it. My job

BASE NOTES

is to work with arrogant arsehole designers who spend all week shouting at me. I put their catwalk shows together, then arrange the aftershow events. It was fun once upon a time, but I'm getting too old for it now.'

'I'd have thought that was a great job to have. Is that why you're in here?'

'Unfortunately, yes. I must lay a floor by tomorrow, so it's a last-ditch attempt to find something that won't rile my boss and complements the clothes. She's a hard woman to please. You know *Absolutely Fabulous*? Edina Monsoon. That's the kind of character I have to deal with.'

'Bet you're never bored, though . . . This one's not bad,' you say, pulling a hidden roll of harlequin tile vinyl from behind the front pile. 'And it's cheap as chips.'

Unrolling the pattern, Tom makes a satisfied sound.

'That'll do just nicely,' he replies. 'Would you like a job?'

'Ha, funny!'

'I mean it. Listen, why don't you come and work for me for a few days? It's in a warehouse down the Meatpacking District. It's quite run-down, but it's the next big area for artists in the city. You can be my assistant.'

For a few moments you fall silent, expressing some gratitude for the serendipity that has just occurred.

'I'd love to,' you say as your volume rises at the compliment. 'Can you pay me? You see, I'm really broke and . . .'

'Hush! Of course I'll pay you. How about a hundred dollars a day? Food. A driver. And anything else you need.'

'It's a deal. But can you get me some cocaine as well?'

Rolling his eyes, Tom nods before agreeing to your demands.

'Oh, that's your *thing* is it? I'm sure that can be arranged.'

*

EARTHWORM

The following morning, you wait on the hostel steps, pushing a salmon and cream cheese bagel into your cheeks. Tom is sending a car to collect and take you to a warehouse, where you'll help him drape fabric from the ceiling and cover furniture for a post-catwalk party. You search for a taxi but can't see one, then notice a black stretch limo has pulled up by the kerb. The window retracts and the driver calls your name. Tom has sent a rapper's car to collect you. Making a loud squeal, you are barely able to conceal the excitement, and roll into the car's back seat.

'Is this really for me?' you ask, incredulously.

The driver, who bears more than a passing resemblance to Danny DeVito, replies, 'According to the account it is.'

Travelling through the city, you wind the window down until you reach Gansevoort Street, where old warehouses are boarded up, with redevelopment signs pasted on fading industrial buildings. Graffiti and litter decorate the sidewalks, homeless people huddle in doorways, with sleeping blankets wrapped around their shoulders. Down here, the streets reek of rotting refuse, leaking engines and turpentine.

Opening the limo door, Tom waves you inside.

'It looks a bit like Manchester. But the boarded-up bits.'

'I suppose it is,' he mutters. 'Now, let me show you around, then we'll have lunch. Can you give me a hand with these boxes?'

You walk up the stairs into a gated metal lift, which takes you to the top floor of a warehouse. An industrial stapler is pushed into your hands. Large rolls of white fabric are balanced against the wall. A cold draught reaches through the window frames as you peer out onto the pavement below.

'By the time we've finished tonight, we'll have draped the entire place,' Tom says. 'We have two hundred votive candles in those boxes, so we need to make sure they don't set fire to the fabric.'

'What time is everyone coming?'

BASE NOTES

'Nine p.m. We have eight hours to make it right. We need fuel. Let's go downstairs.'

You follow him back to the lift, close its concertina gate, then emerge onto the sidewalk, which is cracked and unstable underfoot. Tom leads you through the door of a diner next door, with green and metallic panelling outside and signage saying R&L Restaurant.

'This place is called Florent,' Tom says. 'I think you'll like it in here . . .'

Once inside, you sit with your back against the wall, facing the regulars. The seats are made from cushioned leather, framed maps hang on its panel-beaten walls.

Staring up at the signage above the counter, you squint at the letters.

'Florentissement . . . Trannietown . . . Mineshaftstadt . . . La Toute Petite Belgique . . . Uma Thurman . . . Good Lighting . . . French Fries . . . Single Life . . . Making Star Love in the Night . . . Aeroplanes Fall . . . S&M . . . Chest Hair . . . Miss Meat Market Gown Contest at the Roxy . . . Stomp . . .'

'They have a certain unique approach to menus in here,' remarks Tom. 'Shall we have a drink?'

Although you rarely drink when the sun is up, it seems appropriate at this moment of the day.

'A Sea Breeze, please,' you announce, as if you have the keys to a sophisticated cocktail that nobody has heard of outside of Leeds. 'That's grapefruit, cranberry and vodka. With a lime slice.'

'Sure,' says the waiter. 'We don't need the recipe. What would you like to eat?'

'Hamburger.'

'And the same for me,' Tom says.

'What is this place, anyway?'

'It's open all the time – through the night. And you get a

particular crowd that eat here. It's where all the drag queens hang out, the artists, musicians, fashion people, club kids, that sort of thing.'

You turn left and right, then slowly notice the clientele. Some are dressed in sequins and fingerless gloves, wearing make-up from the night before.

'Agggh. So that's why you brought me here.'

Tom taps his palms on the tabletop, as if he is playing a drum.

'Searching for Warhol. When you told me that in the shop yesterday, I thought you should come. I don't even like his stuff!'

'Fair enough. So what do you like?'

'Joseph Beuys. But he's an acquired taste.'

You have no idea who he is, but Tom starts to recount how Beuys was once in the Luftwaffe and invented parts of his biography, including one tale about being in a plane crash, where a nomadic tribe wrapped him in badger fat and animal fur and saved his life.

Shoving a curly fry into your mouth, you say: 'I like that he invented a story about himself, but the fur and fat thing? That's pretty revolting.'

'Good,' whispers Tom, pushing his finger to his lips, making the sign of silence. 'The best art isn't supposed to be palatable.'

By nightfall, the warehouse is dressed to perfection, and you and Tom frantically light the Santeria candles along corridors and into the venue as a sound system cranks out the latest fashionable sounds. Before the party begins, you spend an hour in a downstairs bar with a giant mirror ball above the dancefloor. The DJ plays a seventeen-minute version of Donna Summer's 'Love to Love You Baby', and you watch the moving lights spin across the ceiling, lost in a reverie. As you walk into the toilets, a man with a gurning face, who has clearly been up for a night or two, beckons you into a cubicle.

He mumbles, 'Hey sweetie. Wanna line?'

Nodding your head, you follow him, then he produces a bag of powder, a rolled-up note, and racks out two slugs on the toilet lid. He leans over first, snorting it in one go.

'This is just the greatest stuff, baby!'

'What is it?'

'Just wait and see . . .'

Then you kneel, with the damp toilet floor residue soaking into your trousers, and imbibe the remaining line up your right nostril until all sense of smell evaporates.

'Ugh. That's foul,' you cough. 'But thanks anyway. Generous of you.'

'Can you buy me a drink?'

Wiping powder from your nose, you pout at yourself in the restroom mirror before replying to the man, who is sweating profusely behind you.

'Right then. Fair's fair. What do you want?'

'Long Island Iced Tea.'

His eyes are almost rolling into the back of his head, but you agree to his tax, and stagger out into the bar, waiting for the chemical cosh to hit. The round costs a substantial amount of the day's earnings, but you hand the glass to him, before collapsing into a chair. The man wanders out into the night, clutching his drink as if it is the Holy Grail, and is never seen again. You are convinced he has crushed up a couple of Tylenol in an attempt to keep up his free drink intake, a tactic, which, you must concede, is an admirable tourist shakedown.

A large crowd of fashion people have started gathering on the streets. Some are Hollywood A-list celebrities, others are Britpop

EARTHWORM

stars. Tall, slender models gracefully walk through the warehouse, and you are captivated by their features and lithe limbs. The supermodels are not like any women you have ever seen, they are mannequins rather than human beings. You recognise the living dolls from glossy magazines, they are the ones who advertise perfume. With physiques of almost skin and bone, you stare at their shoulder blades which poke through their clothes, and their ribcages which form a rack through the soft fabric on their chests. Yet still, although in an advanced state of starvation, there is something transfixing about them.

Sitting alone at the party, you watch catwalk models dance with graceful movements, in thousand-dollar clothes, and realise you have come a full circle. You are by far the worst dressed person in the room, wearing high street rags, and for once, feel proud for not fitting in.

As the crowd swells and the music plays, you leave the party and walk past Florent's café, staring at the unobtainable hipness of those who are eating inside, resolute that no matter how hard you try, you will never be admitted to their ranks. The air is filled with traffic fumes, and the faint scent of Earthworm, which is stuck to your leather wristbands.

Walking away, towards the Hudson River, you head for the slow waves by the side of a pier and listen to their hypnotic lapping sound as the water's glittering light illuminates your face.

BRUT

Fabergé

Engine oil beneath his nails. Swarthy swagger. Euthymol breath. Page 3 stunners. Soap-on-a-rope. Perms and mullets. Darts and snooker. Pints of bitter. Something for the weekend. Keegan and Gazza. Aphrodisiac. Reclining seats. Cock of the north. Rolls of tenners down the working men's…

You have an appointment at 5.30 tonight, which is, you believe, a peculiar time to have an interview. Earlier this week you spotted a 'no qualifications required' advert in the newspaper's jobs column and rang the number out of curiosity, from the call box in town. A woman called Viv said you had a clear manner on the phone and that the position didn't require a formal interview. There was no need to wear a special outfit or bring a CV – she knew who was suitable for the job after a few minutes of talking on the telephone. The role, wages and hours would be discussed. You were given an address and the number of a buzzer to press. Viv would be waiting for you in the office.

After walking along a side street, dodging brown puddles, you stop at a doorway and press the buzzer. Lights are being switched off in the building, on the floors above, and a group of cleaners pass on their way to work. One turns towards you on the front steps, hand on her hip. She has a weathered face pulled back in a harsh ponytail and scrunchie but is probably younger than she appears.

The cleaner asks, 'You all right, love?'

'I'm fine. Just here for an interview.'

'Not the first this week, let me tell you that. You'll be wanting buzzer D, by the way.'

'Thanks. My stomach's going already.'

Shaking her mop from a metal bucket, the cleaner pushes her back against the heavy glass door.

'Good luck,' she laughs. 'You'll be needing it working up there . . .'

BASE NOTES

The building's top floor is part of the attic space. It is bright with neon strip lights that brighten cheap desks with no sign of regular sitters. There is an absence of plants, pictures or pen pots. Not even a folder or notepad. Just a line of grey chairs, each with a grubby telephone facing towards the concrete bulk of the swimming pool outside. The L-shaped room has an ominous atmosphere that makes you pause for a moment.

At the far end of the office, women are conversing on the phone. Some squeal with their feet on the desk in front of them. They all wear earpieces. You listen to their voices, which sound exaggerated; raspy, confident, seductive. Most of the staff are fake laughing as though they are hosting the world's greatest party. It sounds like they are drinking champagne, not litre bottles of Irn-Bru.

You take a deep breath and cock your head around the corner. The women look up and one waves from the front. They are wearing house clothes: jeans, big jumpers, no make-up. Some are eating chips from takeaway boxes. They are divided by carpeted partitions. Most are smoking. Some have jumbo crisp packets on their desks.

A glass wall with vertical blinds is beyond the front office, with a wall of monitor screens playing adverts from different television channels. A black leather Mastermind chair rocks and swivels. You walk towards it with small steps. There is somebody in the chair on the telephone, a fog of smoke surrounds it. The room is dark aside from flashing lights emanating from ad breaks lining the television screens.

'Hello!' a voice shouts.

A small woman with bright red hair and clanking jewellery is walking towards you.

'You must be here for the interview?' the woman says. 'I'm

BRUT

Viv. Now let's get you sat down over here, and you can tell me all about yourself . . .'

Viv pulls out a sheet of paper and asks you to fill in the name, address and date of birth boxes. Her fingernails have extensions with painted scenes on them – tropical islands in the sun. And miniature jewels that sparkle in the office lights. Viv's left wrist has a heavy gold bracelet, beneath it her skin is dark orange, wrinkled like a walnut. The scent of a sickly and overpowering perfume fills the air, it is so pungent you roll the chair back a few inches as your eyes start to run. It is the distinctive haze of Exclamation.

'So, tell me a little bit about why you're here today?'

'There's not much to it . . . I saw the newspaper advert and thought it might be a good way to earn money. I was dressing windows for a while, but they laid me off. Sometimes I work behind the bar at Club Kremlin, though the hours are sporadic, and I keep getting flare-ups. I play records around town as well, but it's not enough to live on.'

Holding up your hands, you roll back the sleeves. The skin is red-raw and cracked around the knuckles.

'Oh dear,' Viv says. 'That does look sore.'

'I could do with a job where I don't get my hands wet. I thought maybe I could try this out and see where it goes. I need one that's a bit flexible but not too far from where I live . . .'

'You mentioned you live close, in Leeds?'

'On the edge of Burley, yes. With my friend. I live in the attic with two mannequins I rescued from the last job. They're terrible company.'

Viv smiles and rocks back on her chair.

'That's interesting. What else do you get up to, when you're not at work? What are your hobbies?'

BASE NOTES

You lean to one side and ponder how much you should tell her. It isn't like any interview you've had before. Qualifications are of no interest to Viv, which is a relief, as you don't have any. Previous jobs are of no concern to her either, which is helpful considering you've been sacked from most.

'Music. Films. Books. That sort of thing.'

'Ah. We have a few callers who are DJs. Now, before we go on, I need to ask you something . . .'

There is an extended pause as she scribbles down a few words without looking up.

'You're twenty-three, right. Do you have a boyfriend?'

Staring back at her, you start to pick at your hands, which are itching under the desk.

'That's a bit of a funny question to ask.'

'Yes, it is,' Viv says. 'I'm only asking because if you come and work here, you'll be on nights. And that means you might need to give up some of your social life to talk to men on the phone. So, what I mean is, if you have a boyfriend, do you think he'd be bothered about that?'

Your cheeks burn red as you take a deep gulp from the glass of lukewarm water on the desk.

'Well, not at the moment I don't. It won't be a problem. I've plenty of friends who are boys but no actual *boyfriend*.'

'You know me as Viv. But that isn't my real name. You don't need to know what I'm really called. In fact, you don't need to know the real names of any of the women on the chatline, because we all have new names . . . we do this to protect ourselves, so that the men who ring up the line never find out who we are.'

'Does that mean I need a new name?'

'Yeah, but you might also want to play a few characters on here, to shake things up a bit. Stop yourself getting bored. It's up

BRUT

to you. See her at the back, with the brown curly hair, eating a doughnut . . .'

Viv points to the woman as she waves back.

'That's Tina. But only for tonight. Because she gets sick of being Tina. That accent's supposed to be Essex, but it's not very convincing . . . she sounds more Australian if you ask me.'

Clicking a number on her phone, Viv puts it on speaker setting. You can hear Tina talking to a male caller on the line. She is right, it's a dreadful accent.

Ooh, yes, I was a model back in the eighties. A top-shelf magazine, don't you know? These days I struggle to find a bra big enough to contain them . . . Yes, I do have a thing about men in uniforms, especially policemen with their big truncheons. Would you like to try yours out on me?

Viv interrupts and leans over the desk.

'Now, the thing about Tina is, she's a bit silly, but the men think she's hilarious. Which means they keep ringing her up. And the whole reason for doing this job is to keep the men talking. Keep 'em laughing, keep 'em entertained. Make 'em think that you might be interested in taking things further. Make 'em think that one day you could be their girlfriend. We're just a fantasy version of what men really want. If they knew what we looked like in here, they'd put the phone down. We invent stories for them, a woman their wives and girlfriends will never know about. See, it's all about the questions you ask . . . there's an art to it.'

Tina is perched on the edge of her chair, pushing her tongue into the edge of her mouth, rolling her eyes as the words come out. She is clearly unimpressed by the erotic conversation and beckons to Viv, making a hand gesture which is perhaps an indication of what is going on down the other end of the phone cable.

'I shan't bother putting that one on speaker,' Viv says.

The women in the office erupt into hilarity as you shuffle uncomfortably in the squeaking seat.

'How does it work, then? You know, like the job. What are the hours?'

'If your trial goes well, then we'd be looking at three nights a week. Twelve-hour shifts, nine pounds an hour. Initially from eight p.m. until eight a.m. One has to be a Friday or Saturday night, as that's when we get the most callers.'

'Why's that, then?'

'Adverts. You know after about ten p.m., they run programmes like *Eurotrash* on Channel Four . . .'

'Ah, right. After the pubs kick out? Naked Germans of the Week and Lolo Ferrari.'

'Exactly that,' Viv replies. 'Well, we run adverts for a few hours. Short and sweet. Pick up the lonely folk who didn't pull that night and are a bit tipsy . . . and often a bit randy . . .'

'And I have to talk to them?'

'That's about it. Some of them have their own *interests*, which I'm sure you'll find out about in time. We have our regulars, of course. There's one who calls every Thursday night from his office. He's a solicitor who has a fetish for electrical equipment, in particular broken kitchen toasters that have caught fire.'

Raising one eyebrow, Viv crosses her legs, making a low groan from the base of her throat. A loud laugh escapes from your mouth in return.

'What does that mean? How does it work?!'

'He just wants to know about how you set fire to the toaster that week, told in your most tantalising, sensual way. That's all there is to it. A simple request. Then he . . . pleasures himself . . . which you can mute of course . . .'

Unable to comprehend the economics of the occupation which you are about to embark upon, you ask, 'How do you make money from this?'

Viv sighs, stands up from her chair, and rattles her key chain.

BRUT

'Follow me,' she says.

You walk towards the glass-walled office as she knocks on the door.

'Alan, can we come in?'

The chair spins around from the darkened room as an older man with spectacles and a cheap Burton suit leans forward with his hand, ready to shake yours. His hair is the same colour as his skin and fingernails, a deep shade of nicotine.

'This is the new girl. She's just trying out,' Viv says. 'Can you show her an advert?'

Alan grimaces like a jackal who has stumbled on a lone gazelle calf in the desert.

'Well, well, well. A newbie. Would you like to see what this is all about, then?'

He taps his hand on the wooden desk, a walnut frame, coated in green leather.

'Don't be shy,' he says in a gravelly smoker's intonation hewn on the mean streets of Castleford. 'Sit yourself down.'

Picking up a remote control, he points it at a big screen by the door. The volume blasts and makes your ears crackle.

'This is the latest, straight out of the can as we say in the trade . . .'

'Make sure you pay attention,' Viv says. 'This is the advert that runs this week, on your trial shift.'

The screen goes blank and Day-Glo numbers begin to flash. A loud cheesy rave tune kicks in with pianos and drum machines, then a Yank voice starts singing 'Come on call Chit Chat! 0898 99 76 69' through a loudhailer. On the television set girls dance in a nightclub, with strobe lights, soft perms and cocktails. And a crowd of people with hands in the air writhe on a dancefloor. A young woman runs her tongue over glossy red lips and sucks on a curly straw. 0898 flashes three times on the screen. In small print, crammed at the bottom is a business address and postcode, and the words 'this is not a live service but allows callers to leave messages for each other'. And the price, of course: 50p a minute.

'What do you mean by it not being live?' you ask.

'Was just going to tell you about that,' Viv replies. 'You see, when someone calls, they listen to the introductions, such as "I'm Viv, just been out in Doncaster tonight, and now I'm at home, looking for a bit of fun. Leave a message if you want to talk. I'm lonely."'

'And then what happens? Do they leave a message?'

'Indeed,' Alan interrupts. 'They think you're a caller, love, just like them, that's the trick. They don't know we exist in here. As far as they know, you've been having a night out and fancy some company. It's your job to keep them on the line, take them to another world.'

He winks, then leans back into his chair and pulls on his waistline, loosening the gape in his shirt. Dark hairs from his belly poke through the buttonhole.

'So do we have to leave a message back for them, and they reply to that?'

'Well done, Sherlock,' he says, rubbing his hands together. 'But you have to talk, for as long as possible. After ten minutes of keeping them going they get the privilege of talking to you live, then the call connects through. After this point we've already rinsed them out for a fiver, but you have to keep them on, be interested in what they have to say. It jumps to a pound a minute after that, so keep asking questions. The longer you keep talking the more money you'll earn. Tailor-make it. And even if they're plonkers, which I'm sure many are, you have to make them feel like a king. Like they are the only thing that matters at that moment.'

Alan starts coughing and pulls out a tartan handkerchief from the top pocket of his suit jacket, he rattles his lungs and spits into the cloth. Then he leans over, putting his hand on your shoulder.

'Puff them up,' he whispers. 'Tell them how you just want a bit of fun. No strings. Don't scare them off. Pretend that you've been out and came home alone. Now you're watching TV in the living room and thought you'd give it a try. Think of it as *customer service* . . .'

'But what if they just swap numbers with each other? All the people who ring up, don't they just want to stop paying fifty pence a minute when they speak to someone they like?'

'Impossible. We have screening software, so any mention of that and the message is deleted. No flies on us, lass.'

'So, really there's no chance of anyone meeting up or falling in love . . . isn't that a bit weird? That it's all fixed.'

Putting her arm around yours, Viv beckons you towards a desk with a live headset on the top.

'They aren't allowed to swap addresses either,' she adds. 'The old fellas have to send letters to the PO Box. Which is controlled by us, of course.'

Viv opens the top drawer of the desk with a key. It is packed full of love letters, written in fountain pen ink, and photographs of lonely pensioners.

'This one's for Janice,' Viv says. 'She has quite a fan club. They like her because she sounds just like a young girl; it's really her mimicking her granddaughter. So, she plays up to it and they send her gifts in return: diamond rings, washing machines, expensive perfume. They have no idea she's fifty-seven. And at least it stops them pestering girls at the school gates. When can you start?'

*

The minutes before dawn are always the bleakest of the night,

BASE NOTES

the point when you are desperate to fall asleep, but the desperate need to earn money, and the caller's desperate need to end their loneliness, kicks in. Your body is fighting itself, ready to keel, yet stimulants and economic necessity force your mind awake. And when you do return home, it's already light, so your body doesn't sleep properly, just a few snatched hours replaying the previous night's calls over and over again in your dreams.

After three months of working at the chatline, nightshifts have already started to make your brain capitulate. You can barely tell what is real right now. Dawn will break in half an hour, so you stand up from the spinning office chair, walk over to the kitchen and splash water on your face in the kitchenette sink. There is one caller who you have kept on the line since 1 a.m. If you can keep him talking until 6 a.m., you'll earn enough to move house by summer. There is no other reason to be doing this job. Living without a washing machine or central heating almost pushed you over the edge this winter. There are only so many trips to the launderette you can take. Only so many duvets you can sleep beneath. You are cold to the bone. Inside and out.

At the back of the office, Alan taps on his keyboard as if he is playing 'Great Balls of Fire'. The sound reverberates overhead, and you watch him pull up figures on the big screen. He opens a file for each telephone, tracking the length of call and how much profit has been made from each.

Annette, who you share shifts with, is the regular star performer. Her father was a gospel singer and taught her how to sing. In quieter moments she gives a rendition of church songs, often just before the sun starts to rise. Her singing is sweeter than any you have heard; she could pass for a relative of Aretha or Whitney. It transports you from the drudgery of this existence, helping you believe in a better place beyond here. One day, you swear to yourself you will write about this job. In your imagination, it is a film with split screens like *Pillow Talk*. Two people hiding who they really are from the person they are pretending to be.

'Now then, Ruby,' Alan shouts, as you start to drift off into the deep recesses of your imagination. 'Come in here and have a sit-down. Could do with a little chat . . .'

Known only by the name of Ruby at work, you amble into his office, closing the door behind you. It is the first time you have ever really studied his face at close quarters; it is mapped with lines like an Ordnance Survey pattern of a mountainous region. His hair is thick and curly, with traces of fading Grecian 2000 on the ends. Alan's lungs creak as he brushes dandruff from his beige double-breasted suit. The scent of his liberal dousing of Brut fills the air. Lavender, lemon . . . basil . . . bergamot . . . jasmine, geranium . . . sandalwood . . . patchouli . . . oak, tonka bean . . . vetiver, vanilla . . . coumarin . . . aniseed . . . It disguises his natural body odour, which has the pungency of a man who gambles too much.

For the past few months in your new career as a chatline hostess, you have slowly accumulated a following. You have invented a life story for Ruby, and now *she* has friends across the country who call up for her on weekend nights. As a result of Ruby, there is almost enough money in your bank account to move to the capital, which is the greatest of all carrots at this moment in time.

'I'm putting together the sales chart for this month. As you know, it's important for us to achieve targets.'

'Oh,' you say. 'Am I not doing very well? It's not for lack of trying.'

'On the contrary, I'm absolutely delighted to see your name so high up on the graph. Look at this.'

Pointing to a large green block on the screen, Alan strikes the end ball of his Newton's cradle, which is placed on the edge of his desk. A small photograph of his fourth wife is framed beside it. He tells you it was taken on their annual holiday to the Seychelles.

'See this, this is your line. You manage to keep them talking. I mean, you aren't Annette or Janice . . . yet . . . but I have a feeling it won't be long before you overtake them. It's sensational news for the company. And more money for you and me.'

'That's a surprise. Wasn't sure if I was even doing it right.'

You squirm in the squeaky chair as Alan leans over the desk. He picks up his personalised fountain pen with his name engraved in gold and signs his name on a document.

'Right? There is no right. I'm sure you could teach the other staff members a thing or two. I've listened in to some of your calls and you have *quite a way with the gents*. Leading them on like that. It's almost like you're their best friend. Yet you don't give anything away. Shrewd behaviour. A lass after my own heart . . . your mother must have taught you well?'

'I just like to talk, that's all. I've never had much luck in the love department, truth be told. But there are some who call every weekend. One works in Canary Wharf, on the night desk, running computers. I read Tarot cards for him, and we talk. Then there's the farmer up in Cumbria. His wife left him and took the kids. He's got nobody keeping him company at all. Mine is the only voice he hears. It's like I'm his shrink.'

Alan cracks his knuckles and pushes his chest out towards you, the residue of last night's jalfrezi hovering on his breath.

'We reward our staff who show potential here. We wouldn't want you going off to any other rival. And there are a few in this very city already who will be keen to take on a sales talent like you. Looking at this data, well, you managed to keep someone entertained for four hours last Friday. You must be doing summat right.'

'That'll be Shaun. He always calls. When his girlfriend's out at work.'

BRUT

He pauses for a moment and starts to smile, performing a paradiddle on the desk with his index fingers. 'Well! The more Shauns you can get talking to you regularly, the better! That's £120 you coined in, just from one caller. You had three conversations going all night. Music to my ears. As the saying goes, where there's muck, there's brass. You are very good for business. As an incentive I'll add a bonus to your wage this month. How does that sound, love?'

You force a smile and stare up at the slow-motion footage on the TV behind him replaying racing footage frame by frame on the evening news. Jockeys thrash foaming horses to the finishing line as others tumble to the ground.

'Thanks, Alan, I'm very grateful. Could do with the extra.'

Alan moves towards the door to open it and taps you on the lower back, leaving his hand there for a second too long.

'I'll be keeping my beady eye on you,' he says.

Arriving back at the desk you can see the phone is flashing with messages. You sit down and plug in an earpiece, exhaling slowly before playing the first. Listening to the message again, you hover your finger over the reply button and think of a few words to say. This caller has been thrown out by his wife after she read the phone bill. The next one will have come home from a club, high on Ecstasy and wanting a woman to talk to, and the one after that will be a fireman, who lives alone on the Fife coast, desperate for someone, anyone, to listen.

A carton of lukewarm chips coated in salad cream rests on the desk in front of you, alongside a can of Coke, a crushed packet of Cutters Choice tobacco, and a heavily kneaded lump of Blu-Tack that has accumulated a coating of fluff from repeated kneading.

'Only two more months and I'll be free of this place,' you shout over to Annette. 'That's it. I've had my fill.'

L'EAU D'ISSEY

Issey Miyake

A moth sleeps on a ten-tonne temple bell. Falling cherry blossom floats in the wind. Transparency. Iridescence. A sense of belonging. Feather kisses on her feet. Matsu resin. Clear, clean and delicate. Origami birds rest by the lake. Komachi, Yosano, the Tea-Master's daughter. Scented flowers fall from their sleeves...

It is the turn of the Millennium, and you are living in a murky flat with medallion carpets, woodchip walls and mahogany MDF furniture, with your new boyfriend, the first serious relationship you have ever had. You met under a bridge on Old Street through a friend of a friend, and he carried your record box to the bar where you were DJing that night. His eyes were sparkling and you were drawn to his warm, infectious nature. Throughout the night, he listened carefully to the music you played, passing Bloody Marys over the decks, matching you drink for drink. Afterwards, at a party, you drank until sunrise. He played 'Waters of March' as the day broke, and said he'd grown up in South America. His parents were church people and raised him in the jungle as a little boy, then sent him to an evangelical school, where he was forced to speak in tongues. Then he studied art, believing he was destined to become one of the conceptual greats. Now he is working in a bank office. He still aspires to be an artist. Art is the only thing that matters to him. There is no God in the world he exists in.

Your new flat has the cheapest rent in Hackney at £65 a week. Located on the hinterlands of the capital, it is close to the marshes and above a spillover mosque, where teenage boys learn the Quran downstairs and during Ramadan, pray for hours each day. As much as you are experiencing limerence with your first proper boyfriend, who rescued you from the West Riding gutter and brought you to live with him here, deep down you are lonely. His friends are your friends. You don't really have any of your own, not yet. The area of London where you live is mostly abandoned. There is scant entertainment around Murder Mile.

BASE NOTES

To stave off isolation, you spend your spare hours in the library on Homerton High Street. The books have become your friends, in the absence of any real ones. It is the first time you have read properly for five years. Being a habitual stoner replaced any ability to read and remember. But now you have stopped smoking dope, the desire to read has returned. You can't smoke anything at all right now, though, even the smell of cigarettes is repulsive. It has been like this since you fell pregnant, but now you are no longer pregnant, it is one of the side effects that remains. Even the subtle perfume you wear, L'Eau D'Issey, is far too strong to tolerate. Lotus . . . calone . . . melon and freesia . . . tuberose . . . cyclamen . . . peony . . . carnation . . . lily . . . amber . . . musk, exotic woods . . . cedar . . . santal . . . osmanthus . . . All perfumes are unbearable this summer.

London's odour is overwhelming, especially in the August heat: armpits on the tube, unbrushed teeth, overflowing bins, blocked drains, rotting takeaway wrappers, decomposing rodents, dirty nappies, rancid swill-outs from butcher's shops and the belching diesel of Routemaster buses. Your ability to drink alcohol has also ceased. For weeks you could only eat salt & vinegar crisps to stop the constant seasickness of your first trimester, a habit which made you gain a stone at least. Barely any clothes from your wardrobe fit and your hair is falling out. Once again, you are not sure where you are heading, but you are glad the past is behind you. Living in the capital offers the chance of reinvention. Nobody knows who you are, and nobody cares. It is time to start from scratch.

Before moving south, your circumstances were desperate. Peppered throughout your head were small bald patches, the size of copper coins, and one large hole the size of a tangerine from the crown to the nape in your neck. For months you avoided going

L'EAU D'ISSEY

home, and when you finally did, your mother burst into tears, before driving you off to her GP who enquired about how many happy pills you'd been taking each weekend.

'It's not normal to drink half a bottle of vodka each night,' he said, before diagnosing alopecia areata, and referring you to a psychiatric unit.

It was clear you were not built for drinking and drugging, and unlike your friends, who had an eternal constitution for intoxication, your body had started to resist. Eating a packet of Super Noodles each night wasn't the healthiest diet, and when one day you dipped your head under the bathwater, and long hair came out in handfuls in the surrounding pool, you knew it was time to stop. But it would take much more than that, and a further unravelling, before you learnt moderation.

During this chaotic drug year, you were contacted by Billy's ex-boyfriend from Edinburgh, who now worked for a television production company. Craig wondered if you'd be interested in appearing on a show he was making about young people and their illicit night-time habits. At first, you were hesitant, but he wanted 'a strong northern voice' for his first show and knew you had hilarious stories about miserable late-night encounters. You had briefly appeared on screen before, once on a game show and another where you were scooped up in a bar and flown to a foreign country with a group of strangers for a cable channel, as part of a new experiment called 'reality TV'. You owed Craig a favour. He had tolerated you living on his floor for months and never asked for rent. Stoned, mentally ill and perpetually on the edge of alcoholism, you stupidly agreed to it out of a sense of guilt.

After spending the previous night on the sauce, you were somewhat the worse for wear when the cameraman turned up that morning to film you in your bedroom, where you naively signed a release form, fingertips oozing lager sweat and skunk weed. The night before, your mother pleaded with you to change your mind, saying you would regret it. A small part of you said 'do not do this', but you ignored the little doubt that would have saved so much trouble with hindsight. As far as you were concerned, you would be six feet under in no time at all, just like so many of your friends back home, so what you said or how you behaved had no consequence. There was no prospect of ever crawling out of the hole you were trapped in.

For two hours you spoke on camera, elaborating and exaggerating every awful late-night tale you could think of: such as waking up next to a man with chronic acne scars as if a tin of baked beans had spilled on his face, regaining consciousness with your trousers around your ankles in a ditch, countless risky fucks down dark alleyways. Then the wallets you emptied when the men had fallen asleep. All of those men you took hopeless revenge on, perhaps in retaliation for the lack of real love, your perceived unattractiveness, or the bitter memory of shin pads buried beneath the rockery stones. It was all a variation on the truth. But as far as you were concerned, the truth didn't matter, as there would be no viewers, so you acted up each story, sarcastically embellishing each awful and desperate physical act for the screen.

On the day of filming, after the crew had left your house, you packed up your belongings into a suitcase, including your passport, family photographs, jewellery and handwritten chat-line letters from faraway admirers, then padlocked the case shut, before squirrelling it into a hatch in the attic, behind an old panel that would never be found. Then you walked to the nearest park with half a bottle of brandy and your Tarot card sets, poured them onto the grass, drenched them with alcohol and incinerated them until only ashes remained. All traces of the person you once were had to be destroyed. As the cards burnt, your past life burnt with it. The act of immolation and erasure was complete.

For many months you pretended the television show would go away, never to be broadcast. That was until you moved to London, and the show was eventually screened. When it finally appeared, your act of self-sabotage caused a catastrophic internal implosion, and then twice again, when it was repeated.

You refused to watch it out of self-preservation, but in the days following, acquaintances shook their heads in disbelief, dismayed at what you had said. Some had a look in their eyes, as if you were lower than vermin. Any perceived virtuousness evaporated. It was even worse for your family back home, who also had to live with the humiliation of it. Your mother was called names in the street, men shouted at her 'the apple doesn't fall far from the tree' as she queued to get into the bank. Your sister was bullied at school. Your father was understanding, and tried to laugh about it, but you knew it must have hurt him. It was by far the worst decision you had ever made. From that moment on you vowed never to be manipulated by the media again.

The act of being on screen, in your bleakest moments of addiction and mental turmoil, was not something you ever wanted to relive. The shame you experienced was so severe you could barely leave the front door without intense paranoia for many months. Every random stranger appeared to be staring at you. Even a newspaper columnist wrote a tirade, believing you to be one of a cast of cretinous individuals who deserved to meet a graphically violent end. You had no way of addressing that, other than to accept the public scorn of a privately educated journalist and to keep your mouth padlocked for fear of attracting more attention. There was nothing you could say in reply. He was the one who fastened the scold's bridle shut. Adding insult to injury, you had fallen pregnant with a man you hardly knew. The year 2000 was supposed to represent a new dawn, but for you it was the lowest ebb.

*

When you first arrived in London you were fired from two jobs before signing on the dole. The benefits were so low that you struggled to eat or pay any rent at all, and although your boyfriend supported you as much as he could, one night you ate boiled eels bought from Netto's frozen range, with the last few pounds you had saved. It tasted so revolting you could not help but push the gelatinous gloop around the bowl, almost retching at the flavour and ammonia that rose from the bowl. He believed you were being ungrateful, and then you had another argument. The next day you swore you were going to find a job, regardless of the role. Mare Street's Jobcentre posted an advert for a local 'fashion merchandising' role, and you made an appointment, which is how you ended up here, working at Leather Looks, a factory on the edge of London Fields.

The factory where you now spend Monday to Friday each week is a hangar with a floor of sewing machines, and a loft piled high with animal skins. The odour of fresh leather is an appalling, putrid stench that sticks to your clothes, hair and skin. Your boss says you will get used to it over time; all the staff stop noticing it eventually.

Your new job is to receive deliveries, record stock, enter it onto the computer system, then dispatch to various out-of-town retail parks across the country. Around Brick Lane, there are finishing workshops down back alleys that stitch and sew for Leather Looks – shadowy places full of Asian women working on Singer machines, with scant fresh air or daylight. Tailors work on the

L'EAU D'ISSEY

factory floor with seamstresses creating jackets, trousers, coats, hats, belts and handbags from the leather, which is mostly nappa made from lambskin imported from North Africa. Before arriving in London, the skins are dehaired, degreased, desalted and soaked in urine and lime, then bathed in a solution of animal brains and faecal matter from dogs and pigeons, before cedar oil or tannin is applied for colour. There is no wonder you are tormented by the odour.

Your colleagues consist of an eighty-two-year-old woman from Golders Green who runs the payroll with a rod of iron; a permanently glum Polish Catholic who has filled her corner of the factory with houseplants and buffs the leaves with milky fluid every morning; a computer guy with a wonky eye who sits watching pornos in his office all day, and Roy, an old school St Lucian tailor who is kind and funny and measures your head for a sheepskin hat which he makes to welcome you on your first day at work. Another is a Pole, Pietrek, who works off the register. He has purple hair and sleeps in the leather hides upstairs at night. The head tailor is a former Hasidic Jew full of stories from his life growing up in Stamford Hill; he is pithy, wise and opinionated. You are always enchanted by what he has to say.

Sometimes when you are loading deliveries onto the lorry, traffic builds on the street, and that's when tension erupts. You are forced to bite your tongue when drivers become abusive, but today it is hard to keep your emotions in check. After asking politely if he could wait a few minutes until you are finished, a man in a souped-up car revs up his engine and gestures at you. Then, you end up shouting at him after he brutally calls you a 'raasclaat'. He bellows from the car in his language, and you bellow back in yours. Then he waves his arms and threatens to come back, at which point Roy storms out of the factory to calm you both down.

London is a tinderbox in the heat. This angry environment is all new to you.

The irate driver has reduced you to tears, which is not like you at all. From a young age, you had learnt not to cry, to bottle things up instead. Unlike your mother, who sobs over any minor reason, a characteristic you always found embarrassing, you do not express feelings unless forced into a corner. But then occasionally, like today, events detonate in a direction you do not anticipate, and the floodgates open.

As Roy leans over into the man's car and speaks quietly to him, you run back inside the factory as your boss pulls you into the office.

'What's the matter?' he asks, gently. 'You can talk to me. It'll stay between these four walls.'

He closes the door and places a cup of tea on a silver coaster.

'Here, have this. I'm a good listener. You won't know this about me, but when I finish here on a night I work for the Samaritans. This, this is just my day job.'

You blow your nose, then take a sip of sugary tea.

'Sorry about that. I don't normally cry. My mother cries over everything, so I don't. It's a stupid thing.'

He looks at you from across his desk, plays with his Parker pen, then says, 'You aren't her, and she isn't you. But the important thing is that the man outside has gone now and he won't be coming back.'

'Thank heavens for Roy,' you say.

'Yes, he's got quite a history. Never take people at face value. Now, tell me why you're really upset. Are you missing home?'

Wiping runny mascara from your cheeks with a tissue, you blow your snotty nose for the third time.

L'EAU D'ISSEY

'It's all been a bit upside down. The past few months. You see, I left Yorkshire and came here with all these big ideas, then found out I was pregnant and everything went wrong. It was a mistake, so I decided not to keep it, because deep down I knew I didn't want it, and besides, I've no money, or a decent place to live, and, well . . . it's just not for me . . .'

'Parenthood isn't for everyone,' he replies, peering over his varifocals. 'I have a wonderful life you know, but I don't have children, and even though I'm getting old, I don't regret that. Now, listen. If you've been through all of this, and you are feeling upset, do you not think it might be worth talking to somebody?'

'Maybe. I'm weirdly emotional right now . . . it's just not like me. I keep crying when nobody's listening, even in the toilets at lunchtime. My boyfriend doesn't know. I wait until he's asleep before letting it out, then I sob into the pillow until all the upset has drained off and the sheets are damp. Nobody needs to see me in that state.'

'It's fine to do that if you feel better the next day,' he says with a sigh, tapping on his computer keyboard. 'But if it happens every night, then perhaps you could talk to someone. Look, here, I have a number for you . . .'

He pushes a piece of paper over the desk, with a telephone number written on it.

'Give this number a call. They offer counselling and you don't have to pay. And if you need some time off to go and see them then just say, it's really no trouble. I don't want to see my staff upset.'

'Thanks, that's really kind,' you mumble, pushing the paper into your jeans pocket.

'You're an intelligent girl. What's your reason for working here, anyway? This isn't your dream job, is it?'

'I haven't worked that out yet. I mean, did you know what you were supposed to be at my age?'

'I don't think I've ever worked it out,' he replies. 'Look at me, I'm in my sixties, still bumbling along. But it's what I do outside of work that counts. My main love is the theatre. That's what brings real joy. Do you like the theatre?'

'Erm, I don't go much. But I suppose I do like it.'

'Well, I get gratis tickets for the National, I'm a patron. If there's anything you want to see, just say. Have you heard of Chekhov?'

'No.'

The Cherry Orchard is running at the Cottesloe right now. Vanessa Redgrave is in it and her performance is magnificent. I'm sure you've heard of her? I'll arrange seats for you. It will do you the world of good.'

'Are you sure?'

'I insist,' he says, as he straightens his cufflinks. 'Now chop-chop. It's three o'clock and we have work to do.'

You leave the office, sniffling, and return to the shop floor, where you flick through a pile of belted coats awaiting stamps and cellophane wrappers. Although London is a harsh place to be, you are touched by your boss's gesture, and start to think of him in a new light.

As you mark the bundles of leather coats, you lift them onto portable rails, pushing the heavy loads onto a delivery van. An occasional shaft of daylight breaks through the grubby ceiling. You stare over at Maria, who has worked here for thirty years; framed photos of her extended family are hung around her machine desk. Her face has an intense concentrated expression as she feeds leather beneath the needle. She is not a cheerful woman, a fact she has made clear on numerous occasions. But Maria has accepted her role in life. The expectations of womanhood are immovable in her culture, and less so in yours, but the

L'EAU D'ISSEY

same basic rules apply – you are born, become a child, start your periods, become a pretty young woman, then get married, have children, work and save, then comes *the change*, caring for your own dying parents, invisibility, cronedom, ill health, and finally death. Maria is counting down the days to retirement and has a calendar with each date crossed out on the wall beside her.

'Only another 462 days of work and I will be free,' she says.

At 5 p.m. the factory bell rings, and you collect your bags before heading home. After shouting goodbye, you pedal along the main road towards the Empire, passing static traffic along the way, then turn right onto Morning Lane, carefully avoiding sleepy pedestrians who step out onto the road without looking.

When you first arrived in early spring, your body raced with excitement and naivety. Each intoxicated weekend extended into the week, with too many careless nights in between. The intensity of early love faded after a month or two, then you noticed a rising nausea, your periods were absent, as ever. A nurse tested your urine and delivered the unfortunate results in a Whitechapel surgery. It didn't take long to make a decision.

Although you are uncertain about most things, one thing you do know is that you have no interest in joining the motherhood club. Not being pregnant is liberating, a truth you do not dare mention. The sense of relief from its burden is a dirty secret. The weight has lifted from your shoulders, the future is one of optimism. Despite your heightened hormonal state, you know the decision was correct.

The day after you had provisionally booked into the clinic, you called your mother to tell her, and she said, 'If you change your mind, I'll bring it up. I've already looked into adoption.'

Her and Buggles being the parents of your unborn child was enough to make you quietly explode and immediately confirm the appointment. 'I haven't even thought of it as being a baby,' you shouted at her. 'It's just a few cells floating around inside! It's just a pissing tadpole!'

'Don't swear. Besides, you've plenty of time to have more.'

'But I don't want kids. Not now, not ever. I've never wanted them. That's why I'm doing this. The drudgery bored you senseless . . . Why would I want to continue that tradition?'

'So that you will understand the sacrifice I made, that's why.' She then paused for a moment, holding back her words, before saying in the most patronising tone she could manage, 'You'll change your mind one day . . . everyone does in the end. I was your age when I had you.'

In the minutes that followed, a dreadful argument escalated down the phone. She yelled and said she never imagined she'd have a daughter like you, that your words have always wounded her. However hard you try to contain them, they erupt when you least expect it. You can be impossibly cruel when provoked. It is not a trait you are proud of.

Dragging your bike through the downstairs door into the flat, you are careful to avoid the piles of pungent trainers that are stacked carefully in the hallway. The sound of prayer emanates from the ground floor. Carrying the frame upstairs, you roll the bike into the box room. Your boyfriend is working at the bank and will arrive home soon. He has dark, depressive moods that are hard to decipher. Whatever solution you suggest is always wrong, so you have taken to letting him stew on his own. On bad days, it's like you are trapped inside with your stepfather again, whose presence was like an immovable iceberg that fills every gap until you too become frozen and consumed.

Pulling off your leathery work clothes, you boil the kettle, and start opening the mail. There is a letter from the DWP officially

L'EAU D'ISSEY

signing you off, a credit card statement showing a £2,800 debt to Royal Bank of Scotland, and an envelope posted from East Riding. You know exactly whose handwriting it is.

Because your grandmother is religious, your mother could not tell her the truth of your situation, as knowing how you had sinned would result in her never speaking to you again. After hearing about 'the miscarriage' she sent a deepest sympathy card with a long letter detailing how 'it is Jehovah's will' that this happened, and how children are a gift. She writes of her brother, who died aged three from scarlet fever, how her father fell asleep with him on his lap, and the boy died in his arms, although he was too deep in slumber to notice after working all day on the docks. His corpse was cold stiff when he eventually woke. Your great-grandmother never forgave him, but went on to conceive her, a brother and sister, after his death. According to her, you must always try again, for these are the trials of being a woman. Our role is to breed and like Eve, she writes, we must suffer in the process. That is Jehovah's will.

'Oh, fucking great,' you say to yourself. 'Just what I need after a day like this.'

Pouring a spoon of instant coffee into a mug, you take a deep breath and decide not to ring your mother this week after all. The heat of rage is clamouring up your neck, turning it an aggressive shade, just like hers does when she's about to blow. Over the past few years, you have drifted so far apart that you barely know each other at all, and your recent television appearance has hardly helped matters.

Raising a child when you can barely hold down a job felt like a rash decision, one that she would say yes to perhaps, but the opposite of your own actions. Maternity was not a choice she showed much interest in, preferring a lifestyle chasing silverware, and then when your sister arrived, she was mostly raised by a childminder, or even yourself. Your mother bore children because that was what society expected of her, not what she truly desired.

You may have conceived in haste but have no intention of being thrown into motherhood in the same fashion.

In the living room, you touch the remains of a bouquet which she sent after your last exchange of words. The apology card fixed on a wire says: 'Sorry, I love you' on the note. She told you she is still learning how to be a mum and doesn't always get it right. They are white roses, with twists of ivy, gypsophila and blue thistles, that have strangely bloomed for weeks.

HAPPY

Clinique

Eternal self-esteem. Late century tonic. She is confident now. Exuberant. Gleaming. Life's simple moments, a cause for celebration. Breakfast Buck's Fizz in her half-full glass…

Walking along Pentonville Road, you speed up the pace as the sound of a fire alarm wails from a looming nondescript corporate office. Overhead, the skyline is milky from pollution. Clattering and shouting echoes from a side street, as bewildered tourist clusters check upside-down maps and the occasional cyclist hollers at passing traffic. It is almost midday.

By the time you reach the ticket hall, swathes of irate passengers are cramped into the seating area, all exasperated at the late-running trains. There are barely any seats. Each food vendor has an impossible queue of passengers for paltry stale baguettes. Pigeons hover over abandoned Burger King wrappers. Homeless hands reach out from stairwells. You search for your mother beneath the turnstiles. She has travelled all the way from Hull.

'There you are!' she calls from behind, then throws her arms around you, squeezing you tight into her enormous bosom, and refusing to let go for a minute or two.

Her bronze make-up is perfectly applied, blow-dry in place, tint and highlights topped up, nails shellacked and set. On her wrists are three gold bracelets, her fingers laden with rings. She is wearing a matching Per Una dress and jacket that sparkle, with a decorative shawl and open-toe sandals as if it's a day at Ebor Races. The smell of her perfume, Clinique's Happy, has already made its way onto your skin. Apple pippin bite . . . mandarin, clementine . . . green bergamot . . . grapefruit and plum . . . lily-of-the-valley . . . freesia and orchid . . . blackberry . . . rose . . . a cottage garden . . . yellow mimosa, a cloud of touch-me-not . . . amber and musk . . . magnolia blooms . . .

'How was your trip? Did it take long?'

BASE NOTES

Removing her shawl, she sighs, rolls it up tightly and pushes it down into her handbag. 'It's boiling down here,' she replies. 'Must be ten degrees warmer than Paragon. But yes, the journey was fine, aside from the rowdy rugger buggers on their way to Twickenham.'

'It's good to see you. Are those new teeth in the pipeline as well?'

A sheepish expression overtakes her face, before she makes a big smile and pulls her lips apart for you to look at. 'I've to wear this gumshield every day for the next few months, it's pulling the crooked ones back, so they'll be straight like they used to be when I was young and gorgeous.'

'Is it painful?'

'A bit. They ache. Although not like a brace. And barely anyone notices. Eh, you'll be getting yours done next.'

You frown and shake your head, then wince.

'I'll keep mine crooked, thanks. The wonkiness is part of me now . . . It seems like ages since we've seen each other.'

'You haven't even been to the new house. I'm sure you're avoiding me,' she says, rolling her eyes. 'But I haven't been down here for at least five years. I've been so busy . . .'

'Shall we walk to the restaurant?'

'It'll be too far for me. I can't manage, not with my chest as it is . . .'

'Let's get a cab, then,' you reply. 'I'll flag one outside.'

Reaching into her bag, she pulls out a small plastic inhaler that resembles a sex toy, grips hold of it, crushes the tablet inside, then sucks hard, absorbing the medication deep into her creaking lungs.

'That's better, the smog's so bad down here. I don't know how you put up with it.'

Climbing into a cab, she makes a sigh of relief as she wedges into the leather seat.

HAPPY

'Oooof. That's better. I've been on the go since six. Had to get ready properly. Then I drove an hour to the station. That road never gets easier.'

'I'm still shocked you moved back to the coast. You always said you hated it growing up . . .'

'Well, times change. And you two moved away. There was nothing keeping me there. Especially after selling the salon.'

'And the massive tax bill, of course.'

Tapping her hand on the glass, she nods in agreement. 'It had to be paid off. So goodbye spacious bungalow, hello poky terrace house with a leaking chimney.'

'Nice!' you laugh.

'Yeah, real nice!' she laughs in return.

'Luxury in Holderness.'

'Back to square one. Here we go again.'

The cab pulls up at a restaurant on the edges of Clerkenwell, and your mother insists on paying the fare. She pauses outside the building and grabs hold of your arm.

'I can't believe we're actually here. I've been watching it on the telly all year.'

'It's your birthday, so I wanted to treat you.'

Booming loudly as she walks into the reception, she proclaims, 'Look at us, living the life! Just wait until I get home and tell everyone where I've been.'

A familiar twinge of embarrassment washes over you, as quiet conversations in the restaurant break into deathly silence as your mother's volume increases.

'Is he cooking today?' she asks the waiter, who delivers a bottle of tap water to the table.

'Who is that, madame?' he replies.

'You know . . . *him*. Your boss!'

He winces, then smiles with a patient tone that he clearly practises on all diners who have arrived via their television sets. 'Ah yes, Chef is not here today, but you will be looked after by staff he has trained personally. In the meantime, would you like to see the specials?'

'Suppose I should,' she sighs with a slight tone of resignation. 'I'll have to come back another time, in that case. Have you any bread? I'm wasting away as you can probably see.'

'Certainly. I'll bring a selection to the table.'

After ordering, you stumble through the usual family discussions of how everyone is, what's causing upset, who has died in the neighbourhood, and the latest gossip from your mother's friends.

'Gordon's depressed again. Karen's threatened to leave him if he doesn't cheer up . . . Jeanette's had her breast off, but the cancer's cleared up. I wish she'd stop smoking . . . Next door but one, Mrs Clarke, she dropped down dead on the patio . . . there's been hell on with Gary as apparently he's been letting the dog do his business in the neighbour's garden, they put CCTV up and caught it in action. So now they're threatening him with court.'

Nodding your head as she speaks, you start to zone out, staring through the iridescent bricks into the adjoining lounge.

She asks, 'Am I that boring?'

'No. Honestly. I was just thinking about what you said. The dog shit wars . . . hell hath no fury like a turd on the lawn.'

'How are things at home?' she asks, stuffing another ball of bread and butter into her mouth between glugs of rosé wine.

'Same as usual, a bit fraught. Job's annoying, but I won't be there much longer. Five years booking bands and DJs is long enough to test anyone's patience. It was fun to begin with, better than any other job I've had. But, working in nightclubs . . . There's only so many dawn finishes you can take before it starts to lose

HAPPY

its appeal. I've just no interest now. All the bands wear trilby hats and want to be The Libertines. I'm at the end of my tether.'

'So, you haven't had Rod Stewart on, then?'

'Definitely not, Mum. Sorry to break it to you.'

She pulls a disappointed face. 'You always liked music. It's a shame you've gone off it.'

'My hearing's shot. I've got permanent ringing, like the screen power's been left on standby and can't be switched off.'

'There's still time for a hearing aid . . . you can finally look like Morrissey and fulfil your teenage ambition.'

'Exactly my thoughts.'

'Have you applied to university yet?'

'I filled out the UCAS form. If I get a place, I'll hand my notice in. There's three who'll take me without qualifications as a mature student. But I've to send a portfolio in, and they judge it based on the stories I've written. For a year I've been saving, so I've enough to get me going. Three grand already. I could do with a holiday, though, but not with *him* because our excursions only ever end one way: in a week-long argument. He's driving me mad.'

'I can't believe it. A daughter of mine going to university. I'm so proud, honestly. It just goes to show, it's never too late to start . . . You've clearly inherited my intellect!'

'Or Grandma's,' you whisper. 'Imagine what she could have done with her life if she was born now.'

'She went to grammar school, you know. On a scholarship. But she was more bothered about being the perfect housewife. What a waste.'

'Instead, she turned to Jedderising.'

Smiling sweetly, your mother replies, 'And we all know how that worked out.'

A plate of lamb arrives at the table, cooked rare and sizzling beneath her face. 'I can't eat this, sorry,' she says, pointing at the plate. 'Too much blood. I can't eat it if blood follows the knife. It's not cooked right. Can you make it more well-done?'

As the plate is taken back to the kitchen you swill the dregs from your glass, patting wine stain from your lips. You spoon green beans from the dish and start eating a prawn, pea and mint risotto which is steaming your face from below.

'I'm nervous about it,' you cough. 'This big change. It's the first time I've ever done anything for myself. And I keep thinking that whatever happens, if I get an education, then it can't be taken from me. They can take your house, your money, everything else . . . But if I have a degree, well, it's there for ever, isn't it? And it means I've achieved something important. I'm going to study hard, as if it's a full-time job.'

As the bowl of charred meat is placed back on the table, your mother ravenously forks the lamb onto her plate. 'I've no doubt you'll finish it,' she says. 'You've always been able to set your mind to a task, even when you were a toddler. When I was a housewife, before the salon days, I taught you to read and write. Not many kids could do that. And no matter how many books I bought you, it was never enough. You'd read all the children's books in the library at least three times. We didn't know what to do with you.'

'Was I exhausting?'

'You can say that again,' she scoffs. 'And precocious. But you were bright.'

'Like James Harries. The Antiques Boy?'

Your mother starts to roar, 'Not like him, no. Thank God. But your brain ran at a thousand miles an hour. It's funny, because your father always said you'd be a writer.'

In the background of the restaurant, the gentle sound of Blue Note jazz plays and is only interrupted by the clank of cutlery in

HAPPY

the immaculate kitchen overlooking the table where you sit.

Wiping chop juice from her chin, your mother reaches into her purse and pulls out a photo envelope which she passes to you.

'Did I show you the photos from the garden party? I've brought them down. We had a Caribbean theme.'

'Is that Gordon in a Rasta hat?'

'It is! Oh, we did get drunk.'

Then she pulls a face that reflects how secretly proud she was at the inebriated state they all ended up in after sinking a bottle of Captain Morgan.

'Is that . . . Geordie Pete? Blacked up?'

She starts hissing as everyone else in the restaurant stares across. 'He used boot polish, you know.'

'You can't let anyone else see these. Not here. Not in London.'

'Why not?'

'You know why.'

'Since when were you bothered about things like that? You used to laugh when I dressed up as Hitler or the Naughty Nun. They all liked that outfit at the Chamber of Trade fundraiser, believe me.'

Pushing your head into your hands, you let out a long groan that breaks into a chuckle.

'Mother. What am I going to do with you?'

Although there is physical distance between you, the confrontational nature of your younger years has been replaced with contrition, and a slow acceptance of your differences has emerged. Your personalities are similar, with opposing views on how you see the world, and who should run it. Living under the same roof, this was a problem. But now you live 264 miles from each other, your chalk and cheese characters are hardly noticeable. For the first time since childhood, you are finally able to enjoy each other's company. An *entente cordiale* has been reached.

'Don't end up like me,' she says, forking the last spots of potato from her plate. 'I know you aren't right. You don't have to tell me. I just sense when something's up.'

'I feel sick thinking about it,' you reply, sighing through your nostrils as she tries to interrupt, stopping herself speaking until you have finished. 'It's . . . It's been going wrong for a while with him, it feels like I'm trapped by my own cowardice.'

'It's OK for you, but I've no choice,' she blurts. 'I'm stuck with mine. You're still young. There's no point being with someone in the hope it might be all right. The reality is . . . it probably won't. Life's shorter than you think.'

After placing her fork and knife in parallel on the plate, she pulls out her compact and powders her nose, stares across the empty plates and mutters, 'We've both ended up with two moody buggers, haven't we?'

'I'm still scared it might go wrong if I leave. On top of that, going to study. Leaving home. Leaving a proper job, an income. Turning it all upside down. You know I can't cope with stress or conflict, but it feels like I've no choice.'

'Have you still got rats under the floorboards?'

'Not since we got the dog. Next door, there's a French restaurant that never has any customers. It's such an odd place. You've to pay in euros, and the owner always wears leather trousers, and a gluey toupee. It stinks of fish . . . they have this extractor fan that backs onto our backyard, slopping grease over my dahlias. I'm convinced the rats come from their kitchen, pushing up the drain covers.'

'I don't know how you put up with it,' she proclaims, shaking her head. 'We'd never tolerate that up north.'

HAPPY

'At least we have a dog to kill them outright, but before that . . .'

'Oh yes, you told me about the poison.'

Attempting to contain a belch as butter rises up your throat, you release the sound slowly into a serviette. It is the first of many today. Like your mother and grandmother, you are cursed with the inability to digest leeks, onions, garlic, kale, cabbage, broccoli and pears. Healthy food triggers major gastric events, which is unfortunate to those who bear witness to your bloating, burping and distended guts.

'Sorry. Uh-huh. The estate agents sent some bloke round, who put Warfarin under the door lintel. Then it poisoned the rats beneath the kitchen floor. The stench, it was hideous, and filled every room in the house, upstairs and down. We could barely use the ground floor for a week. And then, one day, the stench disappeared. And I came back from work, dumped the bike, then walked into the living room . . .'

'Then what happened?'

'It was strangely dark, and I couldn't work out what was different about the room. The blinds were half-closed, so I reached over, pulled them up, and that's when I realised both windows were entirely covered in bluebottles.'

Your mother starts making a loud howl, shaking and coughing as you pull a sour face.

'Oh, stop it!' she says. 'You've set me off.'

'They were all freshly hatched, like in a horror film. Thousands of them. I picked up a rolled-up newspaper and started splatting them. But they didn't fly off. They were sort of drowsy, still asleep. So I scraped them off the window. It filled half a carrier bag, you know.'

'Thanks for that, you've really put me off ordering the bread and butter soufflé. I'm sure you'll end up using it in one of your awful stories.'

'That's why we got the dog, I mean, after that we needed a ratter. And I love him so much . . .'

'Aww,' she coos, 'I bet.'

'This whole situation is going to be even harder now. Walking out on the dog is worse than leaving my boyfriend. Can you believe it? The past few years have been hard living there, though. And I just can't cope with the situation. It's not fair to pretend I want to stay. It's fake. That's not who I am.'

'Listen to me now,' says your mother. 'I've withdrawn some money from my pension, I don't have much, but I want to help you, so I'm putting it into your account when I get home. You don't have to take it, and you can give me it back if you don't use it, but I want you to know that there's money to help you find somewhere to live, so you have a deposit for rent . . .'

As you hear her say the words, you start filling up, grateful in the knowledge that however bad things have been in the past, she is the one person who always has your back.

'That means a lot. Honestly.'

You hold onto her hand across the tablecloth, gripping it tight.

'Take it or leave it. But whatever you choose to do, don't forget you're only twenty-nine. At least you don't have kids or a mortgage or anything else tying you down. There's no point being with someone because you feel sorry for them, or just to keep them happy. You have to be happy too, don't you? And by the way . . .'

Her 'by the way' always means you are in trouble.

'That MySpace page you have . . .'

'Have you been spying on me?'

'No but yes. That man with the long dark hair . . . he's handsome!'

'Oh, the writer . . .'

HAPPY

'Is that your *friend*?'

'No. He's not that kind of *friend*. I don't have that kind of *friend* right now.'

'Right. Not that kind of *friend* . . .'

'He's just a writer friend. I've never even met him.'

You start to grin, then pause for a moment.

'Mum, shut up.'

'I'm saying nothing,' she replies.

The final course, when it arrives with clotted cream, tastes divine. And you both order a portion, chewing on the golden corners, wishing there was another to come.

'It's almost like a mousse, so light and fluffy,' says your mother. 'Mine never taste like this.'

'I've never even tried to make it. Maybe it's all in the bread. London bread.'

The waiter leans over, placing the bill beneath a saucer in a graceful move. She picks up a tumbler on the table, one designed specifically for the restaurant.

'These glasses are sensational,' she says to him. 'They'd look even better if I was sat on the patio at home, holding it in my hand. I don't suppose you'd let me take one as a memento?'

'Don't ask them that,' you mutter beneath your breath. 'As if they're going to let you take it.'

'I just thought seeing as I've come all this way, they'd let me have it. You know, because I'll tell everyone back home how fantastic it was. Free PR.'

The waiter folds his arms and replies, 'I'm sorry, but the glasses are very expensive, we can't let customers take them.'

She looks at him with a pleading expression, then winks. 'I don't mind paying extra!'

'Sincere apologies. It's against company policy.'

BASE NOTES

You make a large sigh then run an imaginary zip across your mouth, willing her to stop making a scene.

'Wherever you go in life, you must get an upgrade,' she says, holding her head up high. 'Hotels, restaurants, flights, even the train. It's always worth a try. If you believe you're special, then they believe it too. Only the best for us.'

HUGO

Hugo Boss

Young, always hungry. Handsome, refined. Straight out of Harvard. Phi Beta Kappa. This fresh-faced kid knows he's an asset. Convertible car. Lusting for life…

You are both curled up in the long grass on top of Silbury Hill, fieldfares circle overhead. The rich midday light is catching your sundial nose, which has turned a rich shade of carob. His breath is tinged with the scent of Jakemans Throat & Chest, a blackberry liquorice flavour sweet strong enough to damage expensive crowns and remove any trace of nicotine. Yours has the faint residue of blood. You have been ignoring the dentist's messages for a while, ever since romance became a primary concern. It is easier to lock yourself away right now, from healthcare, from friends, from commitments. All that matters is this adventure, which you are taking day by day. You are entirely immersed in early love and your new existence south of the river.

Pulling out a packet of tobacco, you take a long swig of lukewarm Lilt and attempt to make a roll-up as a gentle wind whips up the fragments, blowing dry dregs into the meadows below.

'That was quite something,' he says, zipping up his fly with a broad grin. 'Thought I was collapsing into the earth's core for a moment, being sucked into the centre of the earth. What a way to go . . .'

'Death by orgasm,' you whisper, as the lighter singes rogue hair around your face. 'Not the worst ending . . .'

Pulling his grey hooded top over his head, he draws the tie string together to protect his sore ears from the wind, and the remnants of an impetigo outbreak on his face, then speaks quietly, 'How many people have sneaked through the barrier like this over the years? Look, there's feathers and twigs, coins and candles. Someone must have been up here recently.'

Rubbing at your calves, which are still burning from the

BASE NOTES

129-foot ascent in a pair of useless Adidas trainers that have seen better days, you point at the ridge visible from the grass. 'It's all chalk below the soil, you know. Taller than a pyramid, as well. 2300 BC. And we managed to build this. The whole thing just blows my mind. To think we're sat right on top of it. And to think we've just done *that*.'

*

The first night you met, before this year of turbulence began, you waited for him on a hot, dusty junction and searched for his face in a sea of Goya masks. He was late and lost on the Holloway Road. You had agreed to meet at a gig where a mutual acquaintance was playing live, in the cellar of a nearby sweat pit, the Buffalo Bar. To him, you were a dark, slightly unhinged poet from the northern territory, a woman he only knew from various online alter egos. You wrote under four separate names, almost as if you were working on the chatlines again, performing characters on the page that all contained an element of you, although none were the complete works. You were not ready to put your name to anything. Not yet.

As an HGV roared past, you looked up and saw him walking along the road, with a bounce in his step. He was smaller than you had envisaged, with long black eyelashes and inquisitive hazel eyes. But what really struck you was the smell of him as he came close. Evergreen . . . pennyroyal tea . . . Golden Delicious . . . buttery sage . . . geranium oil . . . lavender sprigs . . . moonlit jasmine . . . sawdust stacks . . . pine resin . . . patchouli . . . grapefruit . . . freshly torn basil . . . the sticky tang of Fraser fir . . . And the residue of Pepto Bismol on his peppermint breath. It was as though he had walked straight out of the forest, a handsome faun from the Greek myths, by way of County Durham. Although he was wearing check skater pumps, you wondered if he had hooves tucked inside them, instead of feet. The effect of standing near him for just a few hours that night was intoxicating.

You had exchanged emails, backwards and forwards for months, and knew him only by his writing, by what his poems portrayed. Now the editor of an online literary fanzine, you stumbled across his writing on a forum and asked if he'd like to submit. What he sent, two poems, contained words that burrowed straight into you. Repeatedly, you reread them, as if there was some code embedded in the letters, encouraging you to crack open each stanza. They were words that brought laughter from the depths of your gut, words that made each cell tingle, words that convinced you this man, who was still a stranger, was one that you had known for a thousand years already. This writer was going to become a person of great significance. How, what or why was not something you could answer, but from that moment onwards, standing outside with him on a sweltering city night, the direction of your life was about to change dramatically.

What drew you together wasn't the written word, your shared humour, admiration of literature, music or art. All of that was peripheral, a bonus, but not the actual core. What drew you together was something more basic, a primal interest that could not be expressed in language. A scent that neither of you could verbalise but could recognise if it were bottled and put on a table in front of you.

You weren't looking for him when he parachuted into your life. And you certainly weren't seeking romance. He landed by accident, forcing an old situation to end, and a new one to begin.

*

BASE NOTES

In the block of flats where your new friend lives, a building he has named 'Club Tropicana', you can often overhear two voluminous drag queens screaming blue murder at each other through the paper-thin walls. Their arguments are explosive, almost technicolour in their obscenity. To argue like that takes effort. It has kept you entertained for months but has recently started to grate. There is a swimming pool in the back garden, which is heated in the warmer months, a leftover from its days as a smarter residence. The pool is often surrounded by older gay men baking on sunloungers, drinking cocktails on Sunday afternoons. There are a few families, an extremely loud woman on the top floor who enjoys fornication of the backdoor nature that you are all privy to, even three floors below, and one stern Irish woman with a mouth like a cat's behind, who wears nylon tabards and pearls each day, sagging tights and a pair of sensible shoes.

The first time you visited Club Tropicana you were greeted on the station platform by your new friend. In his hands were a bouquet of artificial roses and a copy of Henry Miller's *Tropic of Cancer*, wrapped in black paper and gold ribbon, with a bow. He invited you for dinner, where you ate fish wrapped in baked banana leaves and coconut rice. You drank wine, he did not. His preferred substance was one that could be bought from a discreet hatch opposite the neighbourhood's police station for £10 a bag. Afterwards, you walked up through the park towards his flat, as your skin started tingling in anticipation at what was to come.

On the second floor, your friend lives in his studio flat with two draughty sash windows, a double bed, and a glass wardrobe, shattered in one corner. His desk is covered in notepads, CDs are piled around the room, and precarious paperback towers are stacked up each wall. In the corner of the room sits a small colour television that he has held onto since childhood, for sentimental reasons. Beneath his bed are the unpublished manuscripts of seven rejected novels he has written, stapled on top are all the polite 'no thanks' letters from editors and agents he has doggedly pursued. They advise him to keep writing, that one day he will be published. He does not take their rejections for an answer, and already has plotted out the next novel he will write. He stays up late drinking pints of coffee, badgering at manuscripts between paid work. Your friend is a man driven by bitterness and determination. The goat scaling a mountain with no end in sight. 'Anger is an energy,' he jokes, as he clocks up the 55,000 words mark on his latest novel, a reimagining of Knut Hamsun's *Hunger*, told through the voice of Richey Edwards.

As a way of escaping the rowdy neighbours, street kids launching rocket fireworks at his window, and continual police sirens racing towards Camberwell, you have started to drive out of the city each weekend in his rickety Fiat, fleeing the noise, and heading towards a more tranquil landscape. One that does not keep you awake at night. The search for peace and quiet has become your mantra. Which is how you both ended up here, staring out across the Wiltshire planes, on top of Silbury Hill, where cirrus clouds and vapour trails drift overhead.

*

Watching the traffic crawl past on the A4, from the top of the prehistoric mound, you turn and point down towards Avebury, the nearby stone circle, with a village built in the centre, and a road running through the middle.

'Why would you build a road through it? What were they thinking?'

Your friend brushes down his jeans, sheltering his eyes from the sun, which is now beating down, and raises the temperature to a level that demands a shedding of outer layers. Knotting them around your waists, you shuffle down through the grass.

'I don't think I've ever been to a place quite like this,' he replies. 'The pagans had it going on. You've been doing this for how long?'

'Stone circling? Around ten years. Not being able to drive doesn't help. Otherwise, I'd be crossing more off the list. This one's my favourite, though, which is why I thought we should come. Worth it when you get here. It's like a megalithic treasure hunt.'

'Have you tried learning to drive?' he asks. 'It's not easy at first, but once you get the hang of it . . .'

'The last attempt I spent almost two grand on lessons. A guy who looked like Terminator used to turn up and force me out onto the Essex ring roads. By the end, I was totally terrified. It just got worse and worse, until I kept making excuses. I can technically drive, but judging distance is hard. I can't seem to decipher how speed works and that freaks me out.'

'So, you're like Father Dougal, then? With the plastic cows.'

'Exactly that! Now, you wouldn't put him in charge of a car, would you?'

'We should head back down. Grab some lunch. My belly's groaning.'

'The descent is harder than coming up,' you say, tucking your jeans into your tennis socks. 'You'll have to hold my hand.'

Together, you stumble down the grass ridges of the ancient hill, grabbing onto each other as you slowly creep towards the meadow of yarrow, knapweed and musk mallow at the foot of its steep bank.

'Sorry, my balance isn't too good, you'll have to get used to catching me, bad ankle, zero ligaments left . . . I was born clumsy . . . arse first. Not much has changed.'

HUGO

Holding your arm up, he says, 'My parents used to take me up Striding Edge when I was four. Me, my brother and sister, all attached by rope. Then we'd creep across the ledges, in a line. If we weren't camping, we were climbing mountains.'

'We never did anything like that. Didn't even own a pair of walking boots. The last thing Dad wanted was to go walking on his days off, not when he worked on a farm. He'd rather watch the cricket or go fishing on his own. And as for Mum, she'd never get her feet dirty. It was all shopping and fast cars for her.'

'They sound like quite different characters.'

'Total opposites. I'm surprised they lasted as long as they did. It was hard for her growing up a Jehovah's Witness, she had a tough time of it. I think she married young to escape it all. After the divorce, she remarried, but I don't think it made her any happier. Dad lives on his own now, out in the sticks. The coldest house on earth. I don't think he ever got over it, really. What about yours?'

'Ah, well, they were childhood sweethearts. Started dating as teenagers, then went off to university together in Liverpool, around the Cavern Club times. Mam studied maths, Dad, physics.'

'Proper smart, then?'

'I don't think their numerical brains were passed down to me. I failed economics in spectacular style. They were teachers, bought a newbuild in suburbia. It was very stable, lower-middle class. We used to go camping in France. That sort of family. They never argued. Bit of bickering perhaps, but they're still married. Totally part of each other.'

'You're in the minority there,' you say, slowly mounting the fence towards the village.

'Aye, that's true. Me grandpa was a teacher as well, and me auntie. And that's what me cousin does. Mam's dad was a shopkeeper on a council estate in Sunderland. They lived in a flat above the shop. He was a hypnotist in his spare time.'

Jumping over a puddle, you hold hands, making your way towards an avenue of trees, and beyond that, the local pub.

'Were you close to him?'

Your friend lowers his brow and sighs.

'Yes, I was. But it was bleak, the end. He was down, and after retiring from the shop he just didn't know what to do with himself. Poor bloke, he kept walking into the sea, always returning with his clothes wet. Men from that time didn't get help, but he did. It wasn't enough, though.'

'I'm sorry to hear that. Must have been awful.'

'I didn't even know he'd topped himself until I was twenty. Nobody told me, because I was too young. Nine or something. And the day he died, I'd been sick that afternoon at school, so I came home early covered in this rash. These peculiar white welts and pink sores and I couldn't stop itching. Perhaps I was allergic to suicide . . . The teachers sent me home. When I got in, there was this silence in the house, like the air had been sucked from the room. An unforgettable stillness. And my parents' faces had this expression of pain and anxiety, trying to explain that Grandad had died, but not telling me how. He used to lend money to the women on the estate, you know, when they were hard up. And they all came to his funeral. I remember his shop had dozens of motivational slogans fixed above the counter. He kept notes on everything.'

'He sounds like a good man. You must miss him.'

'I think of him often. Maybe we're a bit alike? He had some funny ways. Like eating seaweed with every meal or standing and squatting on toilet seats to aid his constipation. Grandad played a mean kazoo as well.'

'What happened to your gran?'

HUGO

'She found his body. His dentures had popped out on the stairwell. That's what she saw first. But after that, she had another life. And I'm glad she did. She didn't want it to define her, or to spend the rest of her years dwelling on it. She'd tried her best.'

Inside the thatched roof pub, the air in the dining room fills with the fragrance of French fries and vinegar, and you huddle around a table, order hot drinks and flick through thumbnails on your camera.

'You know what happens almost every time I come to a stone circle? After I've wrapped my arms around a stone, some great revelation happens. Almost a release of what's been bugging me. Or I learn something new about myself. I know that sounds hippyish. And I'm not a hippy at all . . .'

Your friend nods, then says, with a sarcastic tone, 'No, you're just a punk, aren't you?'

'Maybe I'm a bit of a hippy, on the inside. Definitely not on the outside, though. That's what counts. You won't catch me wearing a pair of juggler leggings. Who do you think I am? Julian Cope?'

'Now you've hugged the stones, how long before the effect?'

You blow on a large cup of tea, until it is cool enough to drink in one go.

'These things can't be measured in such a fashion, sometimes it's days, or weeks, but a change always comes.'

'Here, get some food inside of you. Then you'll be ready for the shamanic aftershock.'

'Thanks,' you say, pushing a soggy fry into your mouth. 'Wonder if this will stay inside long enough to absorb . . . Look, my clothes are hanging off me . . . It's not for lack of trying . . . I keep eating enough, but my guts are all over the place recently . . . I think I've had gastric flu . . . Or a bug . . . It's been going on for months.'

BASE NOTES

'When we get back, I'll buy you some Supermalt. And takeaways from Rye Lane. Fried dumplings. Ackee and saltfish. Rice. Festival. It'll sort you out, I promise. My ex-girlfriend, she got me into that food.'

'The Jamaican girl?'

'She always said it was the best kind of meal when your defences were low. And she was right. It makes you feel better.'

'I'm starting to look like a hungry sparrow. Illness and romance work wonders for burning calories, don't they?'

Tourists weave in and out of the stone circle, taking photographs of each other, some rubbing their hands over the surface, resting their faces against the rocks. Heading towards the barber surgeon's stone, you stand beside it, as cars race behind on the road. He pulls his digital camera out and takes a photograph of you wearing a neon nu-rave T-shirt with cut-off sleeves, an item donated from the design company where you now work two days a week, writing advertising copy for overpriced trainers, in an office that resembles *Nathan Barley*'s *Sugar Ape*.

'This one's famous,' you proclaim. 'I was reading about this before bed. A barber was passing through when the villagers were pushing stones over as they thought they'd been erected by the devil. And then, it toppled over on him, crushing him in one go. When the archaeologists dug the stone out, they found his body underneath with a pair of scissors and a bag of coins. After the barber stone fell, they didn't pull the others down as they thought Satan had intervened and pushed it over himself.'

'Imagine how beautiful it would have looked before that. Crying shame they were used for building walls. Look at that one, it's almost like it has a face.'

You stare at the stone and squint, then proclaim, 'Pareidolia!

HUGO

I know that word from a poem. It means seeing images in other things . . .'

'Like the Turin Shroud?'

'Yes. Or Jesus in a slice of toast.'

'Humans read too much into everything, don't we? It's why we get upset about silly things that are never going to happen.'

Enthused by your first year at university, you have absorbed each lecture into the marrow. Although academic language is often hard to understand, you spend each spare hour in the library, attempting to learn what words like hegemony mean. Your head is brimming with critical theory, romanticism, theological concepts, dramatic structure, heroic myths and narrative arcs. Compared to your previous factotum life, studying is a privilege. Education has opened a door into a future you hadn't ever predicted.

Holding hands as you head towards the avenue by the roadside, the colour of the sarsen stone reflects the change of the sun's cycle. A pale pink hue turns the yellow lichen in their crannies into a brighter, vibrant shade in the fading light.

Pausing for a moment, you sit down on the grass and knot your shoelaces again.

'What's that on your arm?' he asks.

'Oh. It's a birthmark . . .'

'It's such a strange shape. Almost like a map.'

Rubbing on it, you hold your arm towards him. 'There are two. The big one is the outline of Great Britain, the small one is Ireland. It's like a bodged tattoo removal job. I almost had one done when I was pissed in the nineties.'

He starts to smile, tracking his finger around the edges.

'You'll be glad you didn't. Otherwise, you might have had a Celtic band.'

BASE NOTES

'Or Chinese writing?'

'Or a These Animal Men tattoo?' he replies.

Breaking a smile, you pull him close and plant a soft kiss on his neck. He is by far the wittiest man you have ever met, not one day passes without both of you collapsing at each other's observations.

'I've had such a sweet day with you,' he says. 'I mean, it takes some dedication to want to have sex with a man with impetigo.'

You try to stifle a guffaw, then fail, as he points to the scab on his forehead, which you have quietly ignored for the past few days. Leaning forward, you push your head next to his, imbibing the last traces of Hugo Boss sprayed on his shirt.

'It's a bit of a beast, isn't it?' you say. 'Sod's Law you've caught a medieval disease. But what kind of cunt would I be if I refused to see you and cancelled our date because of that?'

'I'm supposed to be at Reading Festival reviewing all those awful bands. But instead, I'm here. With you. At least it gave me a get-out clause. I mean, a lot of people could've been infected at Reading if I'd gone. And they'd all know where it came from.'

'You aren't infectious now, though. It looks worse than it is.'

Pulling his keys from his rucksack, he walks to the car which is parked on a muddy verge. 'I swear I caught it from the nursery next door. It must have floated through the air and into the garden. The joy of Peckham, eh?'

As he starts the engine, you move out into the slow train of traffic, and away from the megalithic site. Pushing a Fisherman's Friend into his mouth, he starts to accelerate.

'Can't we just stay out here, in the fields, for ever?' he says. 'I think I'd like that.'

For a moment the thought of leaving the city crosses your mind, before you are reminded of the bleak midwinter conditions, the lack of money, the lack of work.

HUGO

'Somewhere like this, perhaps. But definitely not the north. We parted on bad terms. I swore I'd never return.'

Overhead, the sky starts to dim, turning a milky shade, as the warm haze of the M25 appears on the brow of a hill. Joining the serpentine chain of red brake lights connecting to the junction, you watch the last dregs of the day fade from view. As your eyes start to droop the FM frequency chops and changes as you crawl on towards the city. The car smells of motorway fumes already; you are still sixty miles from home.

DUNE

Christian Dior

Asleep in the sand drift. Seeking serenity. Dusky pink cheeks. The wild sea roars. A natural woman; dynamic, generous. Shingle paths on a high spring tide. Escape the troubles of modern life. A beach hut, a brolly, a cold case of wine. She touches the golden-horned poppies, softer than admiral wings, and watches her children run to the pier. Driftwood, marram grass, a path of furze-heath…

It is a luminous day, the sort of weather that blesses the North Sea with an unusual sense of tranquillity and calm. Earlier, you walked to the beach with your sister for a blast of fresh air before the funeral service began, and the water glittered in front of you, as if the surface was coated by Swarovski crystals. A touch of sparkle and glamour to send your mother off. The offing had never looked so bright.

Your sister is wearing a long black and white dress, a squirt of Escentric Molecules' 02 perfume and a pair of large sunglasses. The fragrance mimics ambergris, the precious substance found on beaches, the one expelled from the gut of a whale, the one worth more than gold.

For six months, her unborn daughter has been gestating, but the evidence is hardly noticeable. Your outfit is a black cocktail dress, buckled heels and two small squirts of Bvlgari's Jasmin Noir, which today is providing a barrier between yourself and the rest of the world. Before the service commences, you slip a dihydrocodeine tablet into your mouth and swill it back with a bottle of lukewarm water.

'This should blot out the pain,' you say to her. 'NHS heroin. Just what the doctor ordered.'

'I've had a migraine for three days,' replies your sister. 'Not looking forward to this, at all.'

Tradition rules at the oncoming service. Your mother's funeral is complete with Victorian rituals, prayers, hymns and stiff upper lips. As the only scribe in the family, you have written the eulogy. Your words break the ice and make the congregation laugh, as you detail her anarchic escapades over the years. It is the only time you feel useful in family situations, knowing that your role is to write the correct words for weddings and funerals, or find a suitable text to commemorate the day. Three rows behind, your father is sitting alone in a velvet blazer, too hot for midsummer. You wish you could hold his hand right now.

To try to distract from the depressing nature of the ritual, you and your sibling spend secret moments oscillating between your usual sardonic putdowns of anyone who doesn't meet your exacting standards, hidden tears, and gallows humour which always arises between you at unsuitable moments. Today, entertainment comes from being picked up from your mother's house in a funeral car to travel fifteen feet to the church next door (to which you reply: 'We'll walk, we're not that fat!'), then the sight of Uncle Keith turning up to the service in a pair of shorts, which your deaf grandmother mishears as 'the priest is wearing shorts!', and the irony of throwing gerberas onto her coffin as she's put in the ground, a flower your mother always loathed as only *common people with no taste* would buy them.

To find humour at her funeral is something both you and your sister know she would have approved of, even if nobody else does. It is your way of feeling connected to each other, and to her.

'It's the first time I've ever seen Grandma in a church. I thought she'd spontaneously combust,' you mumble as you walk out in procession behind the pallbearers. 'Jedders won't step foot in any house of worship but their own. She used to boycott family weddings and sit outside in the car. And now look at her, she's got no idea where she is.'

'Even dementia has its benefits,' says your sister beneath her breath as you release an inappropriate laugh. Together, you put your sunglasses on, give each other the longest hug, and both walk out into the dappled shade of a churchyard tree.

DUNE

*

In predictable showbiz style, your mother's illness began on a Mediterranean cruise ship after feasting on lobster and drinking champagne at the captain's table, her own version of the Last Supper. The banquet of crustaceans and cheap fizz was quickly followed by stabbing pains in her gut, and then, a volcanic eruption of vomiting blood by the time she staggered back to her cabin.

As with all medical emergencies on board, the floating doctor quickly arranged a helicopter and she was flown over the waves to the nearest hospital, where surgeons repaired her perforated colon and punctured bowel, caused by a septic hernia that inconveniently decided to explode after the boozy communion.

For a month she slept in an induced coma, kept alive by breathing pumps, drips and dialysis, in a room on the top floor of a dishevelled medical building, on an island between Grosseto and the French Riviera. When you visited with your sister, you scaled the steep steps to intensive care twice a day, where you were permitted to watch over her, dressed in plastic aprons, elasticated bags covering your feet, shower caps over your hair.

Her body was bloated from water retention; and her skin acquired a waxy sheen, as if she were a Tussaud's model. A gown covered her modesty, pipes and tubes inflated and deflated her chest. Even her beloved gold jewellery disappeared on the day she collapsed; her wedding and eternity bands conveniently lost. All that remained on her skin was traces of her going-out perfume, Dune. Lily . . . broom . . . peony . . . rose damascene . . . mandarin . . . bergamot . . . jasmine . . . benzoin . . . lichen . . . amber . . . ylang-ylang . . . vanilla . . . a whisper of musk . . . ambergris trace . . . chips of sandalwood . . .

BASE NOTES

When the English-speaking doctor arrived on the ward, you were reading aloud to her, words from the strange shifting sands of Bruce Chatwin's *The Songlines*, where the ancestors sing the world into existence. Pausing for a moment until you finished the passage, the doctor sat on a chair at the end of the bed, crossed his legs and started to talk. 'She cannot hear you speaking to her,' he said. 'But, you know, if it makes you feel better, you should continue. Would you like to see a psychologist?'

'Why are you asking that? *Je suis désolée. Mon français est très pauvre* . . .'

'In France we take care of the patients' families as well as the patients. It is, as you say in English, holistic. Family and loved ones suffer as much as the patient. They need caring for as well.'

His bald head reflected the late afternoon sun as he leant over the bed to check the day's statistics. 'It is strange that her oxygen is so low,' said the doctor. His heavy eyebrows lowered as he pushed his tortoiseshell spectacles up the bridge of his nose.

'Do you think she'll recover? What will happen to her, in the future?'

Shrugging his shoulders, he stared out across the city's skyline. '*Bien*. We have tried our best, but sepsis, it is very bad. Much of her intestine has been removed. Her obesity does not help. If she wants to heal, your mother must lose weight . . .'

'Thank you for everything you've done to take care of her here. She's very lucky to be alive.'

Clearing his throat, the doctor then reattached a drip to her intravenous line. '*Oui. C'est une femme chanceuse*,' he replied. 'I believe she has a chance. You see her heart, it is strong. Like a bull.'

Outside her window, cerise gardenias danced in the breeze, as the hypnotic cologne of jasmine whipped through the hot vertiginous air. Listening to the whirrs and beeps of her dialysis unit, you stared out towards the shimmering horizon, hoping she would survive long enough to at least make it back home alive.

*

Still under sedation, she returned to England by chartered flight and was transferred to a high dependency ward where, for weeks, she existed in a barbiturate haze. Most days, she was preoccupied with a black dog she believed to be running through corridors on the eighth floor of the hospital. Her words barely audible from a tracheotomy, she would point to the imagined creature that propofol had created. For a while she could not recognise you, her own mother, sister or husband.

Throughout those months, you travelled to the east coast, visiting her by train, where hills flattened into horizontal lines, and poplars swayed by the track. LUFC flags and Union Jacks fluttered in backyards along the way, and the metal railings, clad bungalows and boarded-up Portakabins heading out from Garforth, and on towards the Humber Bridge, became comforting in their regularity. Selby's last flour mills cast shadows on a churning River Ouse.

As August started to fade, you traversed the baked pavements, on towards the hospital, which you'd christened 'Hell Royal'. Most days, you sat quietly in the Eye Hospital's waiting room next door, beneath a display of a morose poet's spectacles encased in glass, counting down the minutes before heading into the foyer, where bleeding handcuffed prisoners were paraded towards emergency wards, or women, freshly wounded from drunken hen parties, staggered into the building, with grazed chins and broken feet. Outside, desperate addicts held out their hands, asking for baksheesh, as sirens echoed through the diesel-heavy air.

It took many months for your mother to regain her mind and

BASE NOTES

ability to speak, or to even comprehend what had happened to her that day on the cruise. Her new attachment was a colostomy bag, then large black clouds appeared on her lungs. 'Oh yes, I've had those for a while. It's not cancer,' she told the staff. 'Just a bit of scarring from the bronchitis I always catch. I can never quite shake it off.'

After being wheeled off for further tests, a sharp-eyed radiographer diagnosed her with an untreatable disease common in tradespeople, namely farmers exposed to grain store dust, builders, painters and decorators, or hairdressers from a certain era. The clouds of peroxide, bottles of perming lotion and decades of using lacquer without air conditioning or ventilation had severely damaged the alveoli, causing irreparable scarring and inflammation. The fibrosis had turned her lungs to concrete, each vessel hardened from the chemicals she had been exposed to in a profession unaware of its dangerous potential.

*

The prognosis was between two to five years of life. A length of time she did not reach. As the rain lashed outside in those bleak winter months, the prospect of seeing her first grandchild born was the only incentive for her to continue living. No amount of planning could prepare her mentally for the slow suffocation of her illness, and although she learnt breathing techniques to prevent panic, it was the image of cradling her daughter's newborn that brought most solace.

Whenever you tried to discuss the subject of crossing the River Styx, she'd always reply, 'I don't want to talk about all that depressing stuff. Can't we talk about other things instead?' Even in her final weeks, when she was suffering and gasping for breath like a goldfish out of its bowl, your mother insisted on seeing the funny side. Through laughter, all previous tensions between you were forgotten; in the scheme of life, they became irrelevant.

As you attempted to say something profound about loss one day, she unexpectedly started shaking with mirth and pointed to the woman in the opposite bed who spent her last hours groaning and breaking wind in the night, before passing to the other side. 'What a way to go!' your mother said, pulling the oxygen mask away from her face. 'I hope I don't die farting like that.'

Only humour could guide her through each day, so together you invented unforgiving nicknames for each geriatric that surrounded her bed, a hobby for both of you in the face of desperation. For as long as your mother could speak, she preferred to use her remaining breath on comical moments, rather than talking about such serious matters. Ignoring death was her prerogative.

'I hope you've asked for an upgrade at the Premier Inn,' she kept repeating. 'Have you told them your mother's dying?'

*

In her final days, much to your horror and bemusement, in an advanced state of hypoxia, your mother, in the peak of oxygen-deprived hallucinations in her hospital bed, pulled out her mobile phone and ordered a Tesco delivery comprising four loaves of bread and twenty yoghurts, followed by a stairlift. Paying on her credit card, she arranged for home installation, before promptly discharging herself, against the nurses' advice. Without a mental health section notice, the staff were not able to detain her against her will, so allowed her to leave the ward. Considering how desperately ill she was, you were confused by her release, but sympathetic to your mother's frustration, knowing how she struggled with the cacophony of the ward.

BASE NOTES

An ambulance drove her out of the city, then onto her office, where she waved goodbye to the girls at work, with a breathing mask strapped to her face, believing herself to be the Queen making a victory lap. Then, once situated in her living room, she refused to lie in the clinical bed that had been arranged for her, preferring to stay upright in her pleather chair with pipes in her nose connected to an oxygen tank turned up to the highest setting. She then ordered a takeaway, where she sat eating a chicken bhuna, knowing it would be her final meal at home.

Being in Hell Royal was too noisy, distressing and uncomfortable for her.

'I want to die in peace, away from the racket . . .' she said.

That night, the paramedics were called, and due to the stairlift, were unable to move her from the top floor of the house. She almost died on the stretcher as they pulled her down the carpeted stairs. Then her heart stopped in the ambulance, and she almost departed by the roadside at sunrise. The drama was typical of her, she was not one to leave without some sort of explosive exit.

When you finally reached her the following morning, she was laid out behind a curtain in A&E, wheezing and delirious.

'What are you doing in here, you daft bugger?' you asked.

She stared up at you from her bed, with an evil grin. Even though she could barely talk, her escape from Alcatraz had to be commended.

Sitting beside her bed, you spoon-fed her rice pudding as concerned medics hurriedly attempted to find her a ward, the corridors already full of desperate patients begging for treatment. Mercifully, she did not wait for long.

As her condition deteriorated, she still had hope of a last-minute reprieve, that somehow all you knew about the disease and its grim prognosis could be disproved if she railed hard enough. In her opinion, going to the hospice was admitting defeat, and admitting defeat was not in her character.

Although you always suspected your mother would die young, sixty-three years old was no age to die. You had not expected to lose her so soon, and in such a tragic manner.

*

In those final hours, you were not prepared for the quiet cruelty of watching her fight against the slow death knell of a syringe driver. An animal would not have to endure such a trauma, and you wondered which religious person would believe it humane, if they saw her experiencing such desperation, to deny her a swift and painless ending. Instead, it took three days for your mother to die by end-of-life drugs. Unable to absorb fluids, food or even oxygen, her body had started to fail. If God existed in physical form, he would not allow such a thing, that you were certain of. Even your grandmother told her to stop raging against the dying of the light, but that made her even more determined not to die. Holding on was her last act of defiance, the grand refusal. Until the very end, she believed that willpower alone was enough to save her from fate.

Ice melted in a plastic jug, as rounds of tea and biscuits were brought into the room by sympathetic staff. There was no appetite between you all, only caffeine could propel the spirit. She would not leave the four walls alive. Time ceased to exist. Together, you were all trapped in the bardo. During the first twenty-four hours, she could still almost talk, and ate a bowl of cornflakes, drank a sip of tea; at forty-eight hours her voice had ceased to exist, and on the last day the only communication between you and her was by eyesight. She was distressed and trying to reach you, begging for help, having wet herself beneath the sheets, stripped of all dignity. Even without words, her anguish was clear.

For the first time in your adult life, you prayed, asking the Goddess, Mephisto, Lao Tzu, Buddha, Allah, even your old enemy Jehovah, if any were listening up there in the clouds, to intervene and make it stop. For her, and for all who had to endure the torment. Left alone with her in the single-bed room, there were moments where you considered ending it for her yourself, wondering how long it would take if you put a pillow over her face, and how long you would have to serve over the final act. But in the end, as ever, cowardice won.

As you sat watching the light fade behind her eyes, your sister pushed small sponges into her mouth as her lungs made the unnerving sound of a hundred canaries trapped inside a cage. This was the death rattle you had read about. The view from her room faced south, towards the Humber, and in those numb moments, you focused not on her, but on the river, its silver majesty, and envisaged yourself dissolving into its waters, resolute in the knowledge that all storms must pass.

Some of the last words she said to you, spoken quietly, with an oxygen tube in her nose, are words carved permanently into you. They are words impossible to forget. 'I will always be part of you,' she said. 'Just because my body has gone, the love doesn't stop. It's the only thing that's left.'

ORIGINAL MUSK

Kiehl's

Mystery essence dabbed on the neck. Dopamine hit. Beast of the chase. Euphoria. Restless nights. Infatuation clouding her head...

It is almost 7 a.m. on Boxing Day and you wake to the sound of an air raid siren howling along the valley. Crawling out of bed, you pull a dressing gown on, then walk downstairs. You are greeted by the sight of gallons of water pouring down the back garden, spilling out from drystone walls, and onto the footpath, which has now become a ferocious creek. Opening the living room curtains, you notice a small pool of water inside the front door; so much rain has fallen overnight it is slowly seeping into the house. Moiling clouds hang over the village.

For the previous month it has rained hourly and swings between remorseless fury, sideways showers, fine mist, and raindrops the size of golf balls. Up here in the Pennines, there are fifty words for rain. When it lands on the already saturated soil, with a consistency of a full sponge soaking in the bath all day, it now bounces straight off the surface. Each footpath is covered in gluey mud that makes a sucking sound beneath the boot. There is no place for the water to soak, and no place for the water to head but downhill, via the quickest route possible. As the valley is comprised of a mercilessly steep landscape, the bottom has now started to fill up with water at a rapid rate. Even the canal is overflowing.

Gently, you creep into the bedroom, run a Denman through your hair and catch a glimpse of your reflection. The older and wider you get, the more you resemble your mother. In the wrong light, your face is jowl-heavy, almost like a melting goblin candle. White eyebrows, crooked teeth, bread belly, burgeoning bingo wings. After all these years your nose still appears to be growing. The problem is, beneath the skin you believe yourself to be Joan Collins in *The Stud*, but the reflection which stares back is the other Joan, Joan Sims – queen of puddings, hooked on benzedrine. Now in your fortieth year, there is no denying your resemblance to a matron on a *Carry On* ward.

Pulling on your tracksuit, you lean over your husband's body, which is cocooned in a duvet, and speak gently to him, before heading outside.

'There's been quite a bit of rain. The sirens are going off. I'm taking the dog out to have a look.'

He stirs slightly and groans, 'What time is it?'

'Not seven yet.'

'Ugh. Get back in bed. It's Boxing Day. Can't you have a lie-in?'

'I'm worried. It doesn't feel right. I'll be back soon.'

Within moments, he rolls over and starts snoring like a small bear again. You close the door and shake the dog's lead as you both head outside into the storm.

Down the road, most bedroom curtains are still drawn. Some houses are empty for Christmas. You walk towards the park at the bottom of the hill, which is already flooded to such an extent it has spilt out onto the car park and is creeping along the tarmac. Its murky swill carries remnants of washed-up litter bins, dog poo bags, plastic bottles, and whatever has been lurking in the sewers – wet wipes, tampons, food residue. Already a stench is hanging in the air. The dog stops for a moment, sensing a change in his surroundings, then attempts to pull back towards the house.

'Come on,' you say to him. His sodden terrier ears are already stuck to his face. You watch him shake rain from his coat, then pull him towards the junction. 'This way, good boy.'

ORIGINAL MUSK

Along the road, manhole covers are bubbling and bursting, some erupting entirely as if they were volcanic craters. Behind the Zion Chapel, the steep lane has turned into a river, washing all the loose surface hardcore, cheaply laid after the last flood uphill, down into the drains. And now the drains are blocked, and the water is getting higher.

'I told the council they'd regret laying that stuff,' an old man quips, who is observing the unfolding disaster from behind sandbags in his front garden. 'They never listen to us. It should've been cobbled up there. The Victorians knew what they were doing. Now look at the bloody mess!'

Heading towards a group of women who are surveying the scene, all huddled together in sodden anoraks with their hoods up, you say hello to them.

'Nice morning for it,' one replies. 'What a palaver.'

Another remarks, 'You'll not get far, past here. The main bridge is shut already. They think it might collapse.'

There is a nervous tone to their usual black wit, a sense of humour developed by local women in textile mills over generations, one only truly knowable when no men are in earshot.

As you walk away from them, one calls out behind you.

'Is he still in bed?'

'He doesn't get up before eight,' you reply. 'Part of his beauty regime.'

The women cackle as you head towards the river, through run-off that is covering the bottom half of your wellington boots already.

*

Last night, before the floods began, you travelled back from Salford over the blackening moortops. Inside the car, steam created condensation on each window, as the geriatric Fiat crawled through large ponds welling in each dip of the winding road towards the valley bottom.

Your father sat on the back seat, staring out at the downpour, shaking his head.

He repeated, in astonishment, 'I've never seen weather like this. Look at it! In all my years working outside. This is unbelievable. Almost *biblical*.'

Outside, the village for once was subdued, except for the malevolent storm cloud, one that occasionally groaned, then emptied its contents every few minutes or so, causing the water to rise again.

'How did it feel having a new addition at the Christmas table, Dad?'

'It were just wonderful to 'ave 'er there, you know. She's no trouble, is she? And she looks so much like you and your sister at that age . . . It really took me back . . .'

'I don't think they're getting any sleep yet.'

'No,' he laughed. 'If she's owt like her mother, she won't sleep until she goes to school.'

Since landing prematurely in the week before Halloween, your niece has not slept for longer than an hour and your frazzled sister, although deeply besotted with her newborn, is exhausted in a way you have never witnessed. There are black rings beneath her eyes from the desperate lack of sleep.

'I wish I could help her more,' you said to him, as the car pulled up outside the house, rain bouncing off the windscreen. 'She's been playing white noise through her phone to try and get her off to sleep, apparently the hissing sound is like the inside of a womb. It's hard for her, not having Mum here to help . . .'

'She'll get over it, but it takes time,' he replied. 'There's no preparing for the shock of it. Your life's not the same after the event. Being a parent's the toughest job of all . . .'

*

Walking through the morning rain, towards the bridge, where crowds of bedraggled locals are watching the rising floods, your primary instinct is to call your mother. She would know what to do. Her number is still in your mobile phone, along with the last text messages she sent. You are not ready to delete them yet. Reading her words brings comfort. Her absence is not something you have come to terms with. Each time you experience grief, the emotions are different to the last time. Her presence is still here, just a few metres behind, even today, even in the eye of a storm.

Although there are clusters of locals gathering near the bridge, they are gesturing to you to stay back. The river is rapidly swelling, and running so fast you are in awe of its strength. You consider where this vast volume of water has come from. It has breached onto the main street and is gushing past front doors at a rapid speed.

An elderly neighbour with a harsh chestnut dye-job and badly drawn eyebrows starts chuntering, 'It's the bleedin' grouse moors. The more they burn up there, the less it soaks up. They've that much money they can buy the government off. And nowt gets done. Look at the state of it.'

'There's nowhere for it to go, is there?'

She raises her shoulders, exhales from a vape then points over the bridge. 'Can you see over there? The beer barrels have taken off now. Even the benches.'

Over the water, the pub's metal drays clatter into the bridge, then upended garden furniture, and a floating car, which has turned upside down and is about to smash into the beauty salon across the way. By now, every spectator is at risk. And the dog is shaking so hard he drags you back, panting towards home.

It is impossible to record it or take a photograph; the volume of condensation in the air is destroying the phone's electrics. Along the road, people are frantically banging on front doors, shouting up to all who are still asleep to evacuate and move somewhere safe. As the river rises, so does the sense of panic. There is no assistance from the police, fire brigade or ambulances. Pensioners in sheltered housing are waist high in floodwater. The village is completely consumed by rapids. Overhead, a helicopter hovers in the sky. At least the news channels will have some footage tonight, even if the entire town is stranded.

By the time you reach the junction, the route is severed by the swelling river. You pick up the dog, put him under your arm and attempt to cross the straits. It is so deep it reaches to the knee. Turning back, you manage to wade through to the railway line, where you journey up towards the footpath; all your clothes are sodden with brown sewage water.

Sticking your nose into your cagoule, you attempt to inhale the last comforting traces of Kiehl's Original Musk, a gift from last Christmas that you wear almost daily. Orange blossom . . . bergamot nectar . . . neroli and lily . . . damascene rose . . . white patchouli . . . coumarin seeds . . . a molecule of Tibetan musk . . . The perfume oil sits on the collar of your waterproof, but even that fragrance is barely noticeable compared to the reek of flood-water.

Walking quickly towards home, the park has transformed into a dismal sludgy lake with litter lapping against its waves. The playing field is now under ten feet of water. The only way home is through a path that is already cascading with muck like an open sluice gate.

Sheets of water from collapsed drainpipes run through the

ORIGINAL MUSK

woods behind your house, peeling skin from the ground beneath it. It is soil that hides a multitude of secrets, the site of an asbestos dump in the 1960s which the council has long forgotten about.

Up the steep slope, 200 feet above where you are standing, a small tree topples over, its roots now facing the sky. A car pulls over by the side of the road as two pensioners slam the door and flee from it.

OLD SPICE

Shulton Company

The rugged surfer. Chisel-chinned. Carmina Burana. Wild water rapids. Riding the waves of a thirty-foot breaker. He will become himself. He will find success . . .

Outside his red-brick house, sheets of tarpaulin flap between fallen fence posts, and nettles grow in sheltered corners, beneath the elderberry tree. Leaking freezers, melted dustbins and a rusting wine rack are heaped by the pebledash wall. The shed contains a bike with flat tyres, a lawnmower which hasn't seen light in a decade, and cases of damaged crockery from the old house, long before the divorce.

Wearing a torn boiler suit, wellies and a fleece hat to cover his bald head, your father spends his days carrying seasoned husks of fallen ash, birch, oak and rowan up the farm track, the gales chasing behind him. He drags driftwood from the river's snake-bend, stacking snapped branches in funeral pyres along the banks.

A few days after floods wiped out your own village, the Wharfe's rising water broke Tadcaster's bridge in two. The water coughed up enough debris to cause a fault-line of human detritus that extended across the pea fields: doll heads, Vaseline tins, pop bottles, syringes, children's shoes, rusting shot-cases and stained sanitary towels. Your father spends his afternoons sifting through the litter, collects it into binbags, then hauls fractured tree trunks towards the house, beyond the latticed blackthorn.

The hamlet where he lives contains seven houses. It has a bus stop (out-of-use), a bench, a parish council noticeboard and a road for rat-runners, tractors and joyriders. Along the verges, which are mapped by discarded milkshake cartons and rampant convolvulus, traditionally laid hedges mark the estate boundary. In spring, red kites follow him to the river.

BASE NOTES

When the wind changes direction, the smell from the sewage works drifts into his garden. It mixes with a heavy scent of brewing malt and tractor exhaust fumes. It is sickly; evocative of childhood bedrooms, a sepia smog that hangs over the town, the stench in your hair, clothes and mouth. Live here long enough and you won't notice it.

There's a reason for all this mess. The long days he spends outside, gathering.

'It's cheaper this way,' he says. 'All this for nowt, free hot water. Chopping wood warms you three times: sawing, lifting and burning. Nature's gymnasium . . .'

The house has a back-boiler, no log fire is wasted. His pension would barely cover his heating costs. This is the alternative. Free to those who are fit enough to scavenge.

He doesn't own the house, of course. It's part of the estate, for its workers. Graft and labour in exchange for a roof. Aside from the open fire, the only heating source radiates from inadequate storage heaters first installed in 1944.

Over the years he has learnt to live with the nip. Ice on the inside of windows, a toilet that freezes up. A pantry colder than the £10 fridge that leaks through the floor each August. Damp sheets. Bare floors. Asthmatic coughs as the sun starts to rise. On the front doorstep metal buckets, filled with ash, cool off from last night's fire. Keeping warm is a full-time job.

Not that he wants any pity, it's just how country life is.

You listen to his running commentary as he drags wood along the lane; the useless government, the National League, the loss of everything that once was. But most of all, a nostalgia for how farming used to be. His mother and father, the old ways.

Quiet days are spent in the past, recalling the lost elation of youth. Fights and drinking and women and clubs. Mistakes, bad

OLD SPICE

behaviour and heartbreak rubbed out. He takes comfort in the myth of the man he once was.

Frankincense ... orange ... lemons ... star anise ... spice ... clary sage ... aldehyde ... jasmine ... carnation ... cinnamon ... pimento ... geranium ... vanilla ... musk ... tonka ... cedarwood ... A bottle of Old Spice sits on the bathroom windowsill. Mould collects around its base. You gave it to him in 1996. He is still using it now.

*

Twenty-four years ago, your father moved here, following his foot accident. The doctors advised he would never walk again but a corset, strong will and prosthetics fixed him. He always knew farming was the most dangerous profession. More men killed than in the pits or at sea. It was only a matter of time before something happened to him. Now he walks with an awkward gait, leaning forward, hands clasped behind his back, the only indication of the plastic toes lurking beneath his wellington boot.

Now retired from the farm, shifts in the airline meal factory, even his cash-in-hand castration duties on smallholdings around the area, he chops wood each day as a substitute for the endless toil of his working life, and scrapes by, in his own ramshackle fashion.

Once a month, his friend Baz with NHS glasses held together by Sellotape, and a toothless smile, slices large wood rounds with a chainsaw. As a roll-up hangs from his mouth, oily fingerprints mottle the flavoured cigarette paper. Chopping up piles of oak and ash, they talk in the way only countrymen do; stories of lost limbs, escaped heifers on the A64, the pigman who slit his own throat and bled to death in the sty, their friend who sleeps sitting up and hasn't bathed for a year, the pie trade, slurry pit drownings, petrol prices, tatters stealing gates from the land. They are the last of a dying breed, carrying tales from way back. Stories that have never been written down, only stored in the imaginations and memories of men who tilled the land.

His parents lived here long before he did, before moving into a warden-controlled bungalow. 'Death Valley', as he likes to call it. Your father is superstitious about that place, the pensioners' estate on the other side of town.

'It's where you go to rot,' he says. 'You won't catch me moving down there, I'd rather snuff it out here in the fields . . . The only way you'll take me out of this house is in a coffin . . .'

He shakes his head and continues the repetition of chopping. He's as much a part of this landscape as the trees and barns and cattle grazing grass. Town is no place for a man like him.

A framed picture of his father, holding a bull on a rope by its ring, gathers dust on the windowsill. It was taken at an agricultural show: his Red Poll bull the supreme champion that year. In another faded photograph, the Queen shakes his hand wearing her white spotless gloves; he often sold pedigrees to her. That was the gift he had; the ability to talk to anyone. The gentry valued his cattle, bought semen straws for ten score a shot; he made them wealthy in return. Rosettes and trophies and hundred-guinea calves. Seven-day working weeks. Never the earnings to save for a house. But free milk, eggs and wood for the stove. A whitewashed pantry of curds out the back. For that, the family were grateful. Their deference towards royalty, the aristocracy and landowners was always a puzzle to you, the doffing of caps towards those that kept them in their place, the continuation of a strange sort of serfdom. Yet they viewed it differently, as if they were beneficiaries of extraordinary generosity, being given the

OLD SPICE

chance to live in such bucolic scenery. The truth was most likely somewhere in between.

*

In the living room, three radios are stacked on top of each other, slowly gathering dust. One for football, one for news, the other, a digital, which he hasn't quite worked out how to use. Your father sits on a pile of grubby cushions slurping his tea and belching between mouthfuls. On his feet are a pair of perished slippers that resemble a burst sofa, his boiler suit has a torn flap around his ball sack, with an old hankie shoved in the top pocket.

When town folk think of country people they imagine a wardrobe of plus fours, tweed hats, expensive coats. The reality for most is this: multiple sweaters (with holes), long johns, odd socks, a fleece jacket with a broken zip, trousers held up by knotted blue twine. And a weathered face, the farmer's tan, which deepens each line in the brow. Or fingers stained yellow with iodine, split nails and barbwire-scarred skin.

You listen to him finish the dregs of a mash from his ancient 'Happy Moo-day' mug, as he squints at a three-week-old supplement from the *Sunday Times*. He's been reading the paper for as long as he can remember, his favourite sections being STYLE, and Shelley von Strunckel's horoscopes.

'A good week for Leo,' he shouts. 'Things are on the up. It's a full moon on Friday, best day of the year for luck.'

The mantelpiece is cracked from the heat, where the fire burns all day, every day. You sit in front of it on a one-armed rocking chair, as the logs crackle and spit.

Several years' worth of opened envelopes, crumpled Premium Bond letters and birthday cards from the past decade spill onto the sooty shelf. By his sticky Chesterfield chair, notepads are filled with handwriting legible only to himself. At first glance it could be Cyrillic script. He tells you he is writing a novel based on his life called *The Bullman*, which opens with the line, 'Flags flutter in the breeze . . .' He has written three chapters but is already convinced it could be a bestseller.

Letting any object go is an impossible task; each scrap of paper holds sentimental value. Even your mother's love letters from 1972 are randomly kept in a brown leather wallet, layered with bank statements, mouse droppings, matchday programmes, and shoved to the back of his shed. His hoarding has escalated over time. Already you are anxious about sorting this mess when he dies.

The view from the upstairs bedroom has barely changed since you lived here. At least it has a carpet now, an improvement on the strips of sponge underlay and random nails that lined the floorboards when you first moved in. It was sleeting heavily outside the day you arrived with the removal van. Your neighbour helped move the furniture as your father was on crutches, his chopped-off foot still in bandages. He was a generous but troubled man who worked at the gas board and always shared his B&H cigarettes with you. That day, there was something amiss, an odd mood that you hadn't seen before. For hours you pushed wardrobes, beds, drawers and cabinets into the house, dragging slush and mud from the outside in. All of your possessions were shoved into the front bedroom, facing south. You had finally left home, from your mother's house into your father's out in the fields, where at least the arguments would stop.

'There,' your neighbour said, as he placed a box of records onto the mattress. 'You can play music as loud as you like now, and no neighbours, or your mother, will ever complain.'

OLD SPICE

Putting his arm around yours, squeezing you tightly, he said, 'I will miss you all.'

It was the last time you saw him alive.

From the first night of sleeping here, this house became a sanctuary. Your sagging single bed faced the doorframe, a room that required warming by hairdryer each morning before you could brave leaving the covers, the air so cold you could see your breath.

In this bedroom, a record player sat in the corner, piles of vinyl were stacked against the wall. Music was the only way out, some brief relief from the teenage rut. Back then you earned just enough to get by. Call centres. Pubs. Fitting rooms. Tills.

At night, downstairs, your father would shout at the football on television, it was always the last thing you heard before drifting to sleep. That, and the widow-makers creaking outside.

He looked after you here, in this house. Fed by tins of spaghetti hoops on toast, bulk-bought from Netto as a damaged batch. 30p loaves of white bread. Value packs of watery ham. Own-brand digestives. The occasional Battenberg. That was tea, most nights.

'Always thought you'd be a writer,' he used to say. 'All of them stories you wrote as a kid.'

Wilde. Betjeman. Burgess. Larkin. Golding. Hartley. Steinbeck. Yeats.

Their books gathered dust in a box by your bed.

*

Out here, the stillness is comforting. On clear days, you can see cooling towers on the horizon, structures that once belched out steam. They are slowly being dismantled.

Your father is preserved in time. Even in retirement he's

recreated the daily burden that his body and mind are conditioned to. Slogging is second nature. For as long as he's capable, he will sweat each day until he can no longer lift an axe. The fire in his hearth reminds him he's alive. He dreads the day he can no longer light it.

You walk out into the garden, stepping over the rubble, and walk up a mound of ash, now covered in grass, nettles and dandelions.

'Shall I help you sort this mess?'

He pauses and fills a bucket with damp kindling. His large watery eyes appear to have increased in size as his body weight has declined over the years. Weighing only nine stone and surviving on a diet of beef stew and brown bread, he is slimmer than he was at the age of eighteen. Your father's lithe, sinewy physique carries such little fat that when you put your arms around him, you can feel the bones on his shoulders and ribcage, as if you are hugging his skeleton.

'If you want,' he sighs. 'Best leave it until later in the year, though. I'll 'ave cleared some of it out by then.'

Three faded bath towels flap in the wind, pegged to a rope that runs from hedge to house. It is propped by a corroded stepladder. He pulls a cloth handkerchief from his boiler suit, blows, and wipes the permanent drip from his nose.

'What about the outhouse? It's full of binbags, stuff from when you and Mum were together. It's getting on for thirty years now. You don't need to keep hold of your bills, Dad. There's mouldy books in there, a foot spa, broken ornaments from Nana's house. You don't need all this stuff.'

'I'll get round to it,' he replies. 'Just 'aven't 'ad the time.'

'Maybe we could do a tip run,' you say. 'Clear the beer bottles out. You could do with a new freezer, it's leaking again.'

He rubs his hands and stares out across the fields.

OLD SPICE

'Might see if I can get one off Emmaus,' he says. 'Can't afford 'em new.'

'The last few you've bought have been used and look what's happened to them.' You point at the pile of abandoned fridges stacked up next to the shed. 'It's like Steptoe's yard out here.'

His insistence on paying the lowest amount possible is not only an economic necessity. It's a habit that started as a young man and continues into his seventies. Living frugally, or 'sticking it to the man', is a hobby he shares with many other men of his age, including his younger brother. His one aim in life is to exist on the breadline, even if that way of life causes pain, suffering and physical anguish. He is as close to a hillbilly as a person can get. You call him the Wild Man of the Woods.

Any attempt at restoring a sense of order falls on deaf ears, like it always has done. He'll only clear up the mess when he's ready. And only as long as he doesn't have to pay for it. 'Besides, there's work to be done,' he repeats. 'The fire won't light itself.'

A tractor pulls up outside the house and parks next to the front gate. A clatter sounds from the garden as a pile of pallets are lobbed over the fence. Your father grins and nods his head at the windfall.

'More wood,' he shouts. 'That'll keep me busy.'

RED DOOR

Elizabeth Arden

*A satin bow. Dress pearls, décolleté. Depilation, freckle-bleaching.
Unobtainable perfection. Negligée, peignoir,
silk marabou slippers. Flawless for Christmas. Snow is falling
again…*

On the games room wall of the amusement arcade is a framed gallery of Cassius Coolidge's paintings of dogs playing pool. The glass on each picture is smashed, as if you are witnessing the aftermath of a fight, the air is filled with the odour of recycled chip fat or the occasional cloud of vape drifting in from the street. By the arcade's front door is a claw machine, and from behind the Elvis pinball you watch children striving to win a toy, spending a pound for each Sisyphean attempt. You were that little girl once, and visited here surreptitiously with your grandfather, a man who endured his later years with a smile, a smile that covered a grimace.

Now you are an adult, you are free to loiter on the carpeted aisles of Muggies, eat bags of hot doughnuts for dinner, and spend an hour idling on one-arm bandits, or pushing pennies into the shovel-and-drop machines in the hope of a windfall: Parma Violets, plastic watches, another bag of coppers to feed back into the slot.

Walking up and down the promenade at dusk, you stare out at the horizon, which was entirely black in your childhood, but is now dotted with the blinking lights of oil rigs and wind farms stretching out into the North Sea. This flat landscape, which could easily be in the Netherlands, runs for many miles along the coast, towards the Humber estuary. It is peppered with sound mirrors, caravan parks, nuclear war bunkers and abandoned military forts. A mile out are the underwater remains of forgotten villages that can sometimes be seen at low tide. Out here, the sky is so large it almost swallows you up.

BASE NOTES

As your aunt is away on holiday in Benidorm, you are staying at her house for four nights, where you check in on your grandmother every day at the old people's home, spend time with her and reminisce over photo albums. Between visits you wander the town on foot, which is desolate in early March, spending the odd snatched hour in greasy spoon cafés, where you carefully watch the clientele, observing their behaviour, listening to conversations. 'This place should be a noir crime series,' you tell yourself, before hatching an elaborate plot David Simon would be proud of, and promptly forget it before the night closes in.

This afternoon, before leaving the house, you spent an hour marking papers for the university where you now teach. Then, after drinking a coffee from a machine pod which tastes just like metal, you ventured into your aunt's garage and pulled out the framed family tree, which was once hung in your grandmother's bungalow. Aside from reading books on local history, or the golden age of Hollywood, genealogy was her lifelong hobby, and you cannot look at the tree without thinking of the arduous days you spent with her in local history archives as a child, loading cans of microfiche into the machine, before winding through birth, death and marriage certificates, or newspaper articles that were barely legible.

Those long silent afternoons had a particular fragrance: pencil shavings, furniture polish, paper bags of blackcurrant wine gums. At the time you resented her for taking you there, seeing no reason for the visits at all. Recently, you have started to understand how formative those seemingly dull days were. Your life as a writer and researcher began in those libraries as her unwilling assistant. The family tree a ground source for your overactive imagination. It is only now that you realise its power.

Had she been given the opportunity, or lived in another time, you are convinced your grandmother could have been a writer. A

RED DOOR

Celia Dale, Agatha Christie or Dorothy L. Sayers of East Riding. Failing that, a prosecution lawyer, forensic scientist or crime investigator. Instead, her unrivalled intellect was wasted on trying to be the perfect mother, and even more on the voracious pursuit of God.

*

Spreading 'The Good News' of the forthcoming Armageddon was a dedicated pursuit. Each week, your grandmother gently argued with irritable residents, and you still think of the twitching net curtains and indignant faces that peered through window frames in disgust as people told her to 'mind your own bloody business!' in no uncertain terms. She would always return, smiling, as if she had achieved a bonus by defeat. Each knock on a door would be witnessed, for He was always listening and knew exactly who had been extolling the virtues of faith.

In the comfort of her living room, you earwigged on study conversations, listening to her parrot appalling opinions about Jews, homosexuals, and the role of women in society. According to her, the 'wife's head' was a woman's husband, and all women should be subservient to his views (the irony of your grandfather being the most henpecked of all husbands was not lost on you). For years you accepted her vitriol, until one day *Oranges Are Not the Only Fruit* appeared on the television, and you recognised that the character of Jeanette's mother was, in fact, your own grandmother, and that sort of behaviour was not acceptable. From that moment on, you refused to believe anything that came out of her mouth.

The same could not be said of your browbeaten mother who was raised within the local congregation, with all the rules and regulations of daily life imposed upon her. Some included: no dating without a chaperone, modest dress, Bible study each night after school, and formal baptism. Her only role was to become a wife and mother, supporting the needs of the men in her life. Those who knew her as an adult would baulk at the thought of her obeying anybody's rules but her own. Your mother's libertarian and wilfully anarchic character was not predisposed to the committed theological life. By the age of seventeen, she had started planning covert nights out, concealed miniskirts in wardrobe panels, and chopped off her hair into a savage Julie Driscoll cut, dyed bright orange by her own hand. These transgressions were noted, by your grandmother herself and the congregation's elders, who she regularly reported back to. When the time came to disfellowship your mother, she already had notes in the bank.

One evening in 1969, after putting away dried pots, your mother cracked her head on a kitchen cupboard door, knocking herself out onto the lino floor. When she finally regained consciousness, the doctor asked if she was taking medication, to which she was forced to reply, 'yes, the contraceptive pill', in front of her parents. Within days the elders were informed, a panel of men elected as overseers who administered congregational discipline. Sex before marriage was considered a serious sin and she was forced to face them in a private committee hearing, where she was chastised for her actions. Dating a non-member – which in her case was a fairground boy who worked on the waltzers – taking part in loose conduct, fornication and indulging in improper behaviour resulted in her banishment from the Jehovah's Witness community. She was forbidden from speaking to her Witness friends again; unless she repented, her own future would be damned at the Second Coming.

RED DOOR

For years, she carried this guilt, the shunning hidden inside of her, but the indoctrination she experienced never quite alleviated. She had been raised in a miasma of religious repression that would have consequences for the rest of her life. That you even exist at all is due to the Watch Tower's Worldwide Jubilee of 1975. You were a product of the failed Apocalypse.

Now married to your father, who she met in a nightclub called the Cat's Whiskers on a surreptitious night out in York, she finally escaped her own mother's tyranny, and moved many miles away to live in an agricultural tied house, out in the fields.

Your father, a laidback character, released her from your grandmother's shackles, letting her behave in any way she wanted. He saw no reason to repress her. Married life was the first time she had experienced freedom. If a cake was on the table, she could eat every slice. After a lifetime of being punished by food, she was free to devour whatever she pleased. She was a woman who could resist everything but temptation.

Together, they were a handsome pair. Him, tall, dark and slender, with permanently tanned skin, a distinctive nose and handlebar moustache. She was a reckless, hilarious shipping clerk who loved to shock at any given opportunity. Like him, she had a loud laugh that filled every room, 'fine pins', an enormous bosom and an ample northern bottom, all characteristics your father valued in his cows, let alone his future wife.

Although she had been shunned by the congregation, even after marrying, there was still a sneaking suspicion within her that the end was imminent, a fear that the elders might have been right all along, so she stocked up her pantry with tins in preparation for the forthcoming Armageddon, which was predicted to arrive in 1975. Throughout the year, the slogan 'Stay Alive Till '75' appeared on banners at Witness conferences and became a focus of conversation between her and your grandmother. Both followed the news carefully for any sign of the Four Horsemen. When the End failed to materialise (for the sixth time in the Watch Tower's history), your mother threw caution to the wind and spent the festive period between the sheets, wrapped in your father's arms, as snow fell outside and smoky fires smouldered in every room in the house.

You arrived three weeks late, dry, overcooked and bottom first, a severe breech delivery that ripped your petrified mother in two. It was agreed that you were to be named after a *Coronation Street* writer, Adele Rose, the first female screenwriter on the show who wrote scenes for Bet Lynch, Elsie Tanner and the battleaxes your mother idolised. To give your name a touch of additional pizzazz, an extra 'l' was added, purposely making you suffer the indignity of a name with an incorrect spelling for the rest of your life. It was almost as if she knew what your destiny would be, even before you arrived.

After her waters broke, she was driven by your father to the maternity hospital and was left to labour alone. The next morning, as he signed off the milk delivery on the farm, the doctor performed an episiotomy in the labour suite, a slice that had to be made to drag your body, bottom first, through the impossible hole. It resulted in a haemorrhage of epic proportions. Blood sluiced from your mother's hospital bed onto the floor as beleaguered midwives attempted to stem the ferruginous lake. In the absence of your father, your grandmother arrived and was on hand to set the record straight, repeating to the doctors: 'Abstain . . . from blood.' There would be no transfusion administered as He stated it to be unclean in Genesis, Leviticus and Acts. A book written by His own hand 2,500 years ago was the only knowledge that counted. In your grandmother's mind, there were no rules except His.

RED DOOR

As your mother was wheeled down the corridor for stitches and a plasma drip, your grandmother leant over to her, whispering: 'We'll all meet again on Judgement Day. In the meantime, I'll raise her . . .' She then picked up the hour-old you, and waved your mother off into an oxygen tent, where she fought for her life in the following days, as you slept alone in a line of crying babies, tightly wrapped in swaddling, sweetly oblivious to the traumatic entrance you had endured.

It would be the last time your mother would ever let religion, or her own mother, interfere. For a while, the doctors were uncertain if she'd survive at all.

You were almost made motherless at birth.

*

Pushing your cold hands deep into your coat, you walk towards the lighthouse on your way to the bus stop, standing below its fading majesty, the white paint corroded from relentless salty air. Now the museum opens in spring; inside the café is a bookshelf peppered with your grandmother's history books on the town. They were donated when she moved into the old people's home. The anxiety of its spiral staircase is still locked inside your chest.

Before your mother died, in her cottage five miles away from here, the lighthouse could be seen only from the village rooftops, and mostly faded out behind the cloak of sea fret. Members of the local congregation were informed of her illness and decided to pay her a visit. Your grandmother asked the Witnesses to pray for her. Being a woman of politeness, even in her last weeks of life, she invited them in when they knocked on the door, letting them sit on her sofa, her gasping for breath as they spoke.

'It's not too late to be saved,' they said, informing her of the last-minute reprieve. 'Jehovah will forgive you for apostasy. There's still time.'

For a moment, she considered forgiveness, that essential part of her Christian upbringing, then promptly defenestrated the idea. Looking directly at them, the elders who were dressed in sensible clothes, clinging on to their Bibles, still with the glazed look of brainwashed souls, she replied: 'I was brought up not to be rude, and out of respect for my parents, I'm not going to swear . . . Look at me now, I'm dying . . . My entire life I've carried the shame of what you did to me. You and the others had no right to make me feel I was disgusting, that I'd sinned. If Jesus was here now, he'd help me. But I don't need to repent.'

'We are apologetic about what happened,' they added. 'Times were different then. It's not how we would necessarily act today.'

'It's too late for that. I've carried this in my head for almost fifty years.'

'Prayers will be said for you at the service. Paradise is still within reach.'

'What planet do you live on?' she scoffed, turning her gaze away from them, towards the television, before turning up the volume of *Loose Women*.

'I never want to see you people again. Don't bother knocking. And don't bother praying, either. Do me a favour, shut the door on your way out. And don't ever come back.'

Before arriving to see your grandmother at the residential home, you check your phone, which is beeping from a series of text messages containing links to articles about a virus which is sweeping out of China, towards Europe. Already, there are headlines which are causing concern. Rumours abound that public transport will be shut down, including airports. You do not know if your aunt will make it back in time. Or if you'll be able to leave this seaside town at all. Scant information is known about where the virus came from, only that it is fatal for the elderly, or those who are already ill. In the lodge reception there are requests to clean your hands before entering. Rolling footage of news flickers on television screens overhead.

Walking through the sitting room, which smells of citrus cleaner masking the familiar base note of human-soaked fabric, you search for your grandmother, who is usually here with her friends. Her memory loss was gradual at first, but after setting fire to her kitchen twice at her old people's bungalow, she had to move into care.

Since arriving here, she has had a new lease of life. Karaoke afternoons with her school friends, sherry, tea dances and sing-alongs. The company and laughter she craved. And now she has that, her interest in God has receded. He no longer crosses her mind at all. The trouble, pain and judgement of religion has evaporated. You can finally see her for who she is. The fret of faith is no longer present.

Now in her late eighties, she has mostly forgotten about the Kingdom Hall. For her, the Watch Tower is a long-lost memory, one that occasionally appears in fragmented form, yet holds no succour, power or resentment. Her days are spent quietly watching television: *Countdown*, *A Place in the Sun* and *Come Dine with Me*. By her bed is a pile of sudoku books and copies of *Take a Break*.

When you walk into her room overlooking the car park, she is humming along to an advert playing through her TV screen, sat in her chair, attempting to finish a crossword.

Aniseed, violet, plum and peach . . . orange blossom . . . tuberose . . . clove carnation . . . honeycomb . . . cherries . . . lily-of-the-valley . . . orchid . . . sandalwood . . . jasmine and freesia . . . storax and musk . . . vetiver grass . . . cedar and amber . . .

BASE NOTES

Her barely used bottle of Red Door rests on the windowsill, the perfume she once wore for congregation meetings. Now it is only ornamental.

For the first time in her adult life, there is no Bible by her bedside, only photographs of times past, and mainly your grandfather, the only man she ever loved, aside from *Him up there*.

'Grandma,' you say. 'I've brought you some goodies.'

She looks over to you and pauses for a moment, then calls you by your mother's name.

'It's me, not Angela.'

'Oh. You look so alike,' she replies, before calling you by her name once again. 'Where's my handbag?'

Leaning over her bed, you pick her bag from the floor, and pass it to her. Placing her pens onto a tray balanced on her walking frame, she stares out of the window at people walking past on the street. Above her bed is a large picture of Hull in the 1800s, one drawn as a bird's-eye view from Hessle Road docks. It is a picture you were always fascinated by, as she told you stories of the families who lived there, and her own memories as a child, long before the Luftwaffe's bombs were dropped.

'Shall we go sit outside, get some sunshine?'

'No thanks, I'd rather sit inside. It's *cowld*. Maybe tomorrow . . .'

As the clock ticks above her bathroom, you pull down a photograph taken on your wedding day, framed in brass alongside all the other family weddings. Unlike theirs, yours was not witnessed by an audience. Eloping was the most romantic option, celebrated with fish and chips and a trip round the local charity shops.

Wriggling in her Shackeltons chair, she wipes crumbs from her dress, then shouts: 'That's you, isn't it? Wearing green on your wedding day! Married in green, ashamed to be seen. Have you ever? And orange flowers . . . Where is he today? I've forgotten his name . . .'

'It's Ben. He's in Scotland, writing a book.'

'Have I met him? But you didn't take his name, did you . . . I'm not so far gone to forget that . . . Mrs Stripe, is it?'

'No, Grandma. I kept my surname because I like it. I'm called Dr Stripe now, like a lost Cluedo character in Tudor Mansion.'

'Ohhhhh,' she says with a long drawl. 'A doctor. Fancy that, eh? Aren't you the clever one.'

In the past, this would have only been said in sarcasm, with a bitter note to her words. But today, all the sourness has gone. Her words are genuine.

'Here, have a Werther's, but don't choke on it, otherwise I'll be in bother.'

Reaching out her hand, which is now covered in transparent rice paper skin, she delves into the pink and white bag in your palm, shuffles it around, then pulls two sweets out. Unwrapping the first one, she has the eyes of a child, almost gleeful, at the toffee which is about to roll into her mouth.

'I've not done too well with the puzzles today,' she says, tapping her head. 'It's getting harder, you know. Now what was I saying?'

You pick up the pile of discarded magazines by her bed, and stare at her illegible handwriting. Every puzzle is incomplete, with lines and scribbles crossing out each page. The frustration with her brain is evident. And for once, you feel nothing but sympathy for her. All sense of anger towards the woman has dissipated. It has taken almost a lifetime to let the negativity go. And now, staring at this old lady, who is still spirited, but cannot remember your name, you understand why absolution matters. Because in the end, we all return to dust.

'There's talk of the government shutting down the buses and

trains tomorrow, so I'm heading back tonight. For a few days you'll be on your own. Is there anything you need me to get before then?'

'No, no. This is all fine. They look after me here. Kind, aren't they? I like this room. Where is my handbag?'

For a few minutes you talk, before the tea lady knocks on her door, and brings a cup of watery brew with one sugar into her room.

Holding her hand, you squeeze it, before gently kissing her on the cheek, then walk towards the door.

'See you later, then. I'll be back when it's warmer. I promise.'

'Tell your mum I love her . . .' your grandmother replies. 'And I'll be coming home soon. It won't be long now . . .'

LUNE ROSE

Galimard

Chic academic. A keen observer. Wanderlust tempted her onto the waves. Boat neck shirts, high-waisted trousers. Coral nails, expensive frames. By the harbour, she reads a foreign translation. Coffee cools, she eats fresh papaya. Her younger self, a memory now. Her older self, a far better version. Dishevelled hair, golden and grey. Unfinished books keep her awake...

A jellyfish the size of a clenched fist floats in the dappled waves. You hesitate before peeling off your clothes on the edge of the beach. Behind you, the sunset's yellow haze slowly fades into violet, then grey, as you slip into the wine-dark sea. A superyacht drifts by the bay. Ever cautious, you stick close to the shore, but tonight, a higher force pulls you further towards the depths, where you slowly glide out towards the glistering light of this harvest moon, its face broken only by a stray cloud that cloaks its beams intermittently. In daylight, the water's meniscus is coated by a thin slick of oily sun lotion, but tonight you do not notice it.

On the golden sand, families and friends have gathered to watch the rising pink moon and are quietly chatting and laughing as they eat fried slices from Tupperware boxes. Nightlights flicker into life on the hillside. The occasional scooter engine roars past, breaking the silence, frightening the birds. There is no escaping boy racers, not even here.

Waves lap against the rocks and as you roll onto your back in the comforting waves, the fragrance of fresh thyme from a nearby creek blends with the rich salty air of the Mediterranean. Fishing boats nod on the offing, green parakeets rest in the palm trees above. The smell of this sea is delicate, as is the sensation of swimming through its gentle current. It is not the churning brown version you grew up with. The roaring, violent mass of the North Sea is not one to swim in beneath the moonlight. Your sea is dramatic and treacherous, an unknowable force, a destructive sea that washes villages away, where oil rigs are built, and wind farms blow, with a bitterly cold temperature tolerable for only the hardiest physiques.

BASE NOTES

In her youth, your mother swam in the unrelenting brine every morning before school, throughout the year, competing against her brother, both siblings front crawling through the undertow against a timer. As soon as you were old enough, she insisted you learn how to swim, although unlike her, you refused to enter the freezing pewter waves of the Holderness coast.

Floating with her in the nearby baths, wearing armbands, and a frilly polka dot bikini, as she held your belly from beneath, is one of your earliest memories. Swimming was one of the only physical acts aside from eating, or perhaps what happened behind the bedroom door, that brought her true happiness. Being with her, in the water, was the place where you found harmony together. Two nights a week, she drove seven miles to the nearest pool, and together you would dive for bricks in pyjamas and race each other in the chlorinated waves.

You cannot swim and not return to her in some way. Given half the chance, she would be backstroking alongside you now, saying 'go further, don't be scared', and you would float by each other's side in these clear warm waves, her coaxing you on, despite your natural reticence. It was in these very waters that her illness began, and you think of her now, trapped on the cruise ship, the fear she must have experienced, that last supper, the lobster banquet, before your mind drains of all thought as you slowly return to land.

After reaching the shore, you towel down, and quickly slip into a pair of shorts, painful new trainers, a ragged T-shirt, then walk at speed towards the apartment, knowing that what you have just experienced, out there in the waves, has formed the beginnings of the perfume you will make tomorrow. It will be dedicated to your mother, a fragrance capturing the experience of swimming with her memory tonight. Or maybe it was her ghost. One begins where the other one ends. The scent will contain elements of

LUNE ROSE

your life together. Encapsulating the essence of her. A memoir in a bottle. But not the type she would buy from the shelf, it must dig deeper than that. Now, at least, you know the name of this perfume and the reason why you have travelled all the way to France to make it. It will be called Lune Rose, or in English, Pink Moon. Lune Rose will be a fragrance that symbolises freedom, the future, but not the past. A bottle of perfume to say farewell and embrace the winding road that lies ahead.

At breakfast the next morning, the sun is already blistering your scalp and you wrap your hair into a scarf, tying it into a topknot like Carmen Miranda, before stretching out on the balcony, as your skin starts to tingle at the power of the heat. Jasmine pots grow around the terrace, which emit a strong, unmistakeable scent at night. The streets are full of this same fragrance, which a woman, who walks her chihuahua around the block after dinner, says is called *Cestrum*, a dusk-blooming flower known locally as lady of the night. Its aura is unlike any you have encountered; even your own garden jasmine, which is powerful even in the Pennine hills, smells nothing like this. *Cestrum* is hypnotic, with a sapidity that comes into being as soon as the sunlight fades. That the plant's fragrance is an aphrodisiac with hallucinogenic qualities is not surprising. You decide that jasmine must be in the perfume you will make today, up in the hot hills of Grasse, where the plant is grown in fields, compressed and turned into concrete for the perfume industry.

Staring down at the streets below, the Union Jack is flying at half-mast. French newspapers feature a photograph of Queen Elizabeth, who died a few days ago, on every front cover. There is deference to her, even here in the republic. Unlike most of your family, you would rather turn the Windsors out to pasture. In your radical youth you would gladly have had them all guillotined, yet even today you must admit that her passing has caught you off guard.

When your best friend Steph visited from the Italian border a few nights ago, she came bearing a gift. For days, you had been complaining about the searing temperature, so in return she purchased an offensive fan from a gift shop in the centre of Nice that said *Fuck Off* to mark your forty-sixth birthday. Knowing your penchant for obscene language, the choice was pitch-perfect. She had a matching one that said *Too Fucking Hot*. Together, you decided to take the abhorrent accessories out to dinner, in the finest establishment in the area.

It had been a peculiar afternoon, both of you wondering at what moment the Queen's death would be announced, and where you would be at the time. Huw Edwards was already wearing solemn black on the television news, and for an hour you dialled into the BBC to listen to the running commentary.

At dinner, you devoured fat prawns and parsley ice cream with squid ink mayonnaise, followed by beef, truffle gnocchi and a bottle of red wine to celebrate. Halfway through the meal, you were interrupted by the sound of an opera singer in the square, singing 'God Save Our Queen' with a twinge of emotion breaking the notes. After that, phones pipped on the dinner tables, and the entire restaurant raised a toast. You were oddly subdued as you walked to the seafront, where the Tricolore and Union Jack flags were already lowered, blowing gently in the warm September breeze.

'I best text my brother,' Steph said, brushing sand from her espadrilles as you sat on a bench overlooking the ramparts. 'He should get a big order in for tomorrow. Florists always make a fortune when royals die. When Diana carked it, fucking hell, we were raking it in from the lilies. One bouquet had a card we had to write that said: "Why did you die, Di?" It was delivered to Buckingham Palace. It still makes me chuckle when I think of it.'

'My mother cried for two days. There was nothing she loved more than the Windsors. It's no wonder I turned out like this.'

'Orf with their heads!' yelled Steph, with an element of joy.

As you started walking back to the apartment, a small tortoiseshell cat ran through the traffic and towards you. Pausing for a moment, as it approached, it weighed up the element of risk, and allowed you to stroke it behind the ears. Immediately it started drooling onto the path, lost in a reverie of affection.

'I'd have one if they didn't make me sneeze so much,' you said. 'Didn't you tell me that Lily of the Valley was the Queen's perfume?'

'Yeah,' your friend replied, cackling. 'But that's a different lily. It's funny because we always use them in funeral arrangements . . . I can't stand them. You know it's one of the only flowers that can mask the smell of death?'

'*Très outré* . . . Their stamens make me wretch. I find them unbearable. If a shop has them on display, I must leave. It's the only flower I can't be in the same room as.'

Lighting her fifteenth cigarette of the day, she started to smirk as she recalled her days working on the flower stall, where she made gates of heaven from tiny carnations, or tributes to West London gangsters, such as poker cards, racehorses or even rolled-up notes and piles of cocaine in floral form.

Staring out across the shore, as you reached the edge of the beach she proclaimed, 'My favourite was making CUNT out of roses, for a grandad the whole family hated. One time, I dressed a wicker casket, using wire for the lilies, which people don't like anymore as they're not environmentally friendly . . .'

'Is that when you punctured the corpse?'

Rolling her head back, Steph started to cough. 'Mate! That

never happened. But the hum of a decaying body, I've never forgotten it.'

'What is it like?'

'You instantly recognise it. Death, well, it's incomparable. It smells of only one thing . . . there's no denying that old familiar stench . . .'

You mull over Steph's recollections as you travel through Juan-les-Pins, Cannes and then up towards the mountains; when you finally arrive Grasse, where there is no indication of how to reach the centre of town. You are still carrying her *Fuck Off* fan, which attracts the odd furtive glance on public transport, but in today's heat, you are glad of it.

The ground is radiating heat already, and you conclude that a very steep set of steps is the only likely route towards the centre. Your nose is already starting to burn, so you head towards the cobbled streets, then walk almost vertically up to the top of the hill, grateful that you live in a similar town that requires painful ups and downs for every trip to the shop.

Along the route, murals of perfumers are spray-painted onto the walls, guiding lost tourists towards the promised land. After thirteen years of living in Calderdale, you now have calves like a gnarled mountain goat, and thick, thunderous thighs that can push your body from the valley bottom to the moortops without too much complaining. Last year, you moved out of the dark terrace that was home for a decade, away from the pall, the Boxing Day landslide that backed onto your house, and the eternal misery of nine months without direct sunshine every year, across to the other side of the valley, where the light shines even in midwinter, a place where fruit can grow, vegetables can harden, and the frost doesn't punish the plant life.

Your new garden requires effort and graft. It contains plants

LUNE ROSE

with names you have never encountered: Canadian burnet, bloody cranesbill, dragon's blood, bear's breeches, purple toadflax, globe thistles, wild teasel, wolfsbane, loosestrife, laburnum and fifteen varieties of rose that tangle and climb up the soot-stained sandstone walls. It is a long-term commitment, but you are devoted and have spent many hours with your nose buried in petals, deciphering scents and nurturing each needy plant as the sound of *Gardeners' Question Time* plays from a radio on the broken front step. Being outside, with your hands in the soil, is a great healer, the tending of this garden a protection from the cloying residue of grief.

As you reach the hilltop, the streets of Grasse are sheltered from sunlight by avenues of pink umbrellas, suspended high above in the air. You follow their path, passing perfumeries and patisseries, until you reach the centre, and realise that the place where you are supposed to be heading is two miles in the opposite direction, in the melting afternoon heat.

When you eventually arrive at the Studio des Fragrances, a heady wave of eglantine rolls through the balmy September air. A woman calls your name and leads you into a testing lab, where umber bottles are neatly lined up on curved shelves. English-speaking guests are led into a corner with the Nose, an elegant woman with an immaculate complexion and hair pulled into a bun. She is wearing a white doctor's coat. Before the appointment, guests were requested to not wear any fragrance, or deodorant, as that affects the ability to smell with clarity. After today's panic walk, you catch a warm waft of your own ripening body odour, a hot fox stink, and keep your arms tucked in close.

Sitting alone, you stare up at the selections of bottles on each shelf. A test tube is situated on the desk. To your left you can hear two American newly-weds talking to each other. As part of their honeymoon, they are making a love potion to commemorate their trip and will leave with a bottle wrapped in golden netting and a ribbon tied around the neck. Their accents ring with the up-speak of a younger generation with plenty of 'likes' peppered between sentences: each statement sounds like a question, as if they are permanently perplexed. Unlike them, you are not here for romance or a shared experience, you are here to make a bottle of perfume in memory of your mother. It is serious business that requires concentration.

Placing an empty form on the table, the Nose points to the bottom row of brown bottles that line the lower shelf.

'These are the base notes,' she says. 'Make sure you don't put the bottle directly below the nose, it is better to waft the scent towards you, like this . . .'

In a graceful movement, she rolls the fragrance around the bottle and coaxes the scent towards her nostrils with a cupping gesture.

'Pick out the five you like, then line them up. I will come back and give you the measurements.'

For a moment, you are overwhelmed by the variety of smells that hang in the room; it is almost a bombardment, as if you have walked into a festival with sixty-seven bands playing all at the same time. You concentrate. Then focus. And for the next few minutes, you pull corks off the bottle tops, then waft them beneath your nose, which you have always believed has special powers through its generous dimensions alone.

You select bottles that are appealing – including opoponax, a Somalian sweet myrrh and ancient incense; *accord musc*, a note originally taken from the gland of a musk deer; *bois de santal*, a sandalwood reminiscent of antique shops, and *mousse*, an oak moss, which evokes the smell of the green paddock behind your

LUNE ROSE

father's house to such an extent that one whiff of the petite glass bottle immediately transports you back there.

'Are you finished? Very interesting,' the Nose says, as she looks at the selection and shuffles the bottles in an act of legerdemain. 'I think I know what sort of perfume you will make today.'

Writing down the suggested quantities on the form, she says slowly, 'Follow these measurements exactly, pour the bottle upside down into the tube so you have fifty millilitres of the base notes in front of you. Then, when you are done, pour the formula into this jug, then back into the tube. After that, dip the scent stick into the perfume, and you will be ready for the next stage, the heart notes.'

As you fulfil each part of the process, for a moment you believe this parfumerie excursion is perhaps the most fun you have had in many years. Your excitable feet flap about on the stool as you recall chemistry lessons at school, and your hilarious teacher, from Barnsley, with a black moustache and white hair, who would be delighted that his most hapless student had finally ended up back in the lab, all these decades later.

Pouring out the selected fluids into the tube, you dip the scent strip in and inhale the concoction. It is pleasant, almost earthy, but perhaps too sickly for your taste.

The Nose looms over you from behind.

'You use the strip to smell the other bottles on this shelf,' she whispers. 'Bring the smell towards you via this base note you have made. That way you can tell if they match, or appeal to you.'

Picking up a variety of bottles – *ambre*, patchouli, lichen and *tubéreuse* – you reject them in favour of a blind selection of *océan*, the smell of the sea; *chèvrefeuille*, the honeysuckle of your grandparents' garden; *jasmin*, the scent of Antibes; *air de* Provence, the thyme and herbs that floated in the air of last night's swim; and

BASE NOTES

tilleul, a tincture of the linden tree, once used to treat respiratory diseases in traditional medicine, or the wood once used for making guitars.

When the top notes are finally selected, you opt for *mandarine*, the memory of Santa's stocking, the subtle fragrance of mashed English breakfast tea, lychees, the fruit with a texture of eyeballs that your mother always bought on your secret expeditions, and lotus, a moody floral aroma with a muddy tang, a symbol of strength, resilience, and rebirth.

The large test tube now contains the various notes that are harmonious to you. But they are also a collection of memories and experiences, each element a part of your own personal history, provoking a transportation of sorts. Gently stirring the liquid together, you are convinced that this is a classic scent, and when the Nose gives you an approving nod after imbibing your fragrance, a wave of smug satisfaction washes over your face at the creation.

Before leaving the lab, you are given a pale pink box containing a glass bottle, with a name label attached to the front, and the title of your perfume, Lune Rose, printed in italics. There are garlands of rose and ribbon illustrated on its design, and the image of a woman wearing an apron, gathering fragrance from a compress vat first used in early perfume-making.

You are told you must wait at least six weeks before it can be opened, the components need time to blend, and the longer it is left sealed, the better the scent will be.

Stepping out into the immense late afternoon heat, you hold the bottle up to the sun, shaking its contents as light reflects from its shimmering golden lid.

*

LUNE ROSE

Two months later, winter is closing in. Crowds are jostling to leave the train station, and as you walk onto the packed escalator, you stare up at a talon-less pigeon which is hobbling on the sill, pecking at discarded crisp packets beside you. Joining a long queue for the cash machine, you listen to a group of boys drenched in Lynx Africa playing bassline music through their iPhones, as they talk in a lingo now familiar to you between puffing on pineapple vapes.

As per usual, the day has been subjected to three downpours, even the insides of your pockets are damp. You have been daydreaming about living in the south of France all morning. This is not an experience unique to you: those who live in the Pennines are ravenous for warmth and clear skies. Now the days are shortening, the outlook is grim.

You step over the crossing, and head towards the Odeon. Bradford has become a place you have a deep fondness for. It is a city full of stories; and perhaps the only one where you can observe a wild narrative being played out in front of you – a play, a novel, a film – on any street you turn. There are no dull moments. You have spent many years here as an adult, parading its suburbs, writing about its buildings, its history, and the people. When you came here as a child, you were captivated. This is not a feeling that has ever left you, and even today, staring up at that same sky, burning orange as it bleeds over the rooftops, your senses are heightened within yards of walking along the road. It is the first time you have entered the ice rink since 1984, some thirty-eight years ago.

Back then, the main arena had chandeliers, and you recall the afternoon sun beaming through its windows, dappling the ice as you wobbled reluctantly by the barriers, your mother beckoning you to let go and trust in your own ability. The interior has seen better days, but you are comforted by this lack of change; it is almost preserved in time. Running your fingers along the banister, up towards the ticket booth, you notice the wood still has names carved in by compass. Perhaps they are the same ones from the 1980s and never replaced: 'Dave + Denise', 'Knobhead' and 'Chris Woz Ere'.

After paying in, you lean across the barriers and listen to the swishing sound of scraping blades, and the deranged squeals of over-excited girls on the cusp of adolescence attempting to stay upright. There are ice stabilisers in the form of plastic snowmen and penguins to cling to, the steady hand of a parent surplus to requirements. These are independent children already, wanting to make their own way on the ice.

As the cold starts to nip your fingertips, you walk over to the vending machine and purchase a Crunchie. It is Friday, after all. Each mouthful is a madeleine that immediately transports you back to your mother. There was always a justification for gluttony in her eyes, and even though she is long in the ground, the memory of her is enough to feel as if she is only two feet behind you saying, 'go on, buy it', when faced with whatever is forbidden.

An elderly gent skates slowly, but intricately, in the centre of the rink, as if he were once a champion. He tells you he is eighty-one years old and travels by bus from Saddleworth each week, practising three-turns in a pair of perfectly polished boots with gleaming Sheffield steel blades. You ask him how long he's been dancing. 'Ten years,' he replies. 'It's a very dangerous sport, so I go slowly. That's the trouble these days, people go too fast.' For him, progress is made through mistakes, falling over, diligently rehearsing then learning how to really balance. He has broken his foot and sliced his hand open twice, but it hasn't stopped the determination. 'Patience is an art,' he laughs. 'It gets easier with age.'

There is no music in the rink today, the main sound is the echoing of blades on ice, the salty scratch as twists and turns are

LUNE ROSE

attempted, then abandoned. You are still not tempted to hire a pair of skates and venture out there yourself. Even as an adult, your reticence is obvious, and likely informed by the memory of your mother's broken leg and the chaos that ensued. You think of her during that time, her frustration with the tedium of motherhood, her exasperation with married life, her indefatigable pursuit of silver trophies. All that sparkled gave some relief. Be it diamonds, fast cars or designer perfumes. Risk was a thrill she chased.

Before setting off today, you opened the perfume box from your French excursion with a rising sense of expectation, before spraying Lune Rose onto your wrists and down your neck, in the hope that this remembrance of things past would stimulate the memory of childhood, or the sense of thrill and anticipation you felt back then. Even after a few hours of wearing the fragrance, it has not provided the experience you envisaged in the laboratory. Although it is cold inside the ice rink, you can detect the base notes if you bury your face into the collar of your jacket. It is almost noticeable if you inhale deeply.

Instead of the subtle, evocative scent you expertly crafted, what is present on your skin is something far more downmarket. It is not the precious concoction of your imagination. It is not a perfume your mother ever would have worn. Most certainly not an Alexis Carrington fragrance. What Lune Rose really resembles, if you are truthful, is a brand of cheap copy perfume bought for £3 in the middle aisle at Lidl. It is a disappointment after the grand effort; you acknowledge now that the best laid plans don't always work out.

Rather than pure poetry you have replicated a pleasant floral bathroom freshener. Or a Shake n' Vac that has languished in the understairs cupboard for thirty years. This is not a fragrance that would attract the opposite sex or make you the envy of your neighbourhood. Neither is it a perfume that would embody its wearer with self-confidence, joie de vivre, or the type of aspirational elegance advertised in the pages of glossy magazines. It is a pound shop perfume.

The underwhelming nature of this bottle, after all the effort you have made, would not be lost on your mother. If you listen carefully, you can almost hear her laughing behind you on the bench, rolling her head back, shaking with mirth and pulling a face as she inhales it.

'Not Giorgio,' she whispers. 'And definitely no patch on Rive Gauche. You won't catch me dead wearing *that*.'

A little girl, around the age of eight, with long brown plaits, sits next to you and watches her mother, who is attempting to tie her laces. You see the girl hesitate, as her mother crouches over wearing a denim gilet with a sequinned tiger embroidered on the back. 'Come on,' she mutters. 'You've been nagging me to come here for weeks and now you've changed your mind. I've taken a day off work to bring you here.'

Tension rises between the two.

'I'm going to fall,' her daughter says, with a slow whinging tone to her voice. 'Like him over there. I don't want to . . .'

The girl gestures towards a boy with a mullet who has crashed into the nearby barrier, collapsed onto his shin pads and is now wailing for help.

'I can do my own laces.'

'You always think you can do everything yourself, but you can't,' her exasperated mother replies. 'Why are you being so bloody difficult today?'

She zips up her daughter's fur collar coat aggressively, takes her by the hand, and pulls her out towards the ice.

'Look,' her mother says, pulling her shellacked nails through fingerless gloves as she speaks. 'I'm here, holding your hand. So don't be scared. You need to move into it, like this. It's called *confidence.*'

Her mother skates backwards, then forwards, and bends her knees in a rocking motion.

The girl looks up at her and shakes her head, then leans her body back. She is being coaxed out against her will.

'You learnt how to walk, didn't you? And I taught you to ride your bike. And to swim. So now you're learning to skate. You're a big girl now. Can we stop messing about please, Little Miss Awkward?'

There is a pause, as the girl looks out across the ice rink, the light illuminating her face. She frowns, then starts to talk beneath her breath, her cheeks flushed pink with frustration: 'Mummy. Sometimes, I really don't like you.'

There is a pause, as her mother scrunches up her mouth, so that her lips pucker in an irate way as if they are about to explode.

'Well, sometimes I don't like you either,' she replies.

There is a familiar expression to her face. You attempt to stifle a smile, and quickly stare in the other direction as the mother catches your eye.

She shakes her head, pulls away from her daughter's hand and leaves her standing alone.

You hear the girl whimper, before stopping for the lack of a sympathetic ear. She clings onto the barrier, and then, when her mother disappears into a group of chaotic skaters, ventures out alone beneath the spotlights, realising she is finally able to move on her own.

Staring down at the ice, the girl wonders if her blades will catch on a crack, but it is smooth underfoot, almost like glass, or the surface of a long-forgotten perfume bottle, its fragrance buried many inches down, deep beneath her feet.

Acknowledgements

Sincere thanks to the following people who made this book possible: Lee Brackstone, Sophie Nevrkla, Tom Noble, Jenny Lord, Katie Espiner, Terry Lee, Lucinda McNeile and all at White Rabbit/Orion. My agent, Matthew Hamilton. Copy-editors Kathryn Myers and John English. Helen Meller at Arvon Lumb Bank. The Authors' Foundation at the Society of Authors. The International Anthony Burgess Foundation and the University of Manchester's Centre for New Writing. John Mitchinson at Unbound. John McAuliffe. Carol Gorner and the Gordon Burn Trust. My friends and family: Katy Joyce, Emma Stripe, Lisa Cradduck, Chloé Raunet, Lias Saoudi, Anna Wood. Robert Boulton, Becky Clarkson. Alfie Pickard for her expert research. Gratitude also to Ivan Smagghe for his encouragement.

To my husband, Benjamin Myers, whose suggestions and advice have helped bring some of these stories to life on the page, thank you from the bottom of my stone-cold heart.

Some of the adapted stories in this book originally appeared in the following publications: 'Soul on Ice' in *3:AM London, New York, Paris* (Social Disease, 2008), 'Driftwood' in *Common People: An Anthology of Working-Class Writers* (Unbound, 2019), *Stay Alive Till '75* (Ration Books, 2021), and 'The Beautiful Game' in *AMBIT* (Issue 243, 2021). Poems written between 2006 and 2012 and published in chapbook form by Blackheath Books as *Some Things Are Better Left Unsaid*, *Cigarettes in Bed* and *Dark Corners of the Land*, have been reconfigured and used in various scenes.